ALWAYS
AHEAD

ALWAYS AHEAD

12 Striking Stories of Determination, Commitment, and Inspiration in Pursuit of Success and Freedom

**Contributing Authors
(in order of inclusion):**

*Randy Tipton   Jason Kush   Caleb Spears   Jon Bohm   Craig Boyd
Stuart Crawford   Jeremy Schubert   Jason Boyer   Lauren Bailey
Elaina Verhoff   LaDarren Landrum   Rick LaRue*

OLEG BORTMAN

Published by Best Seller Publishing®, St. Augustine, FL
Best Seller Publishing® is a registered trademark.
Printed in the United States of America.
ISBN: 978-1-962595-42-1

This publication is designed to provide accurate and authoritative information
with regard to the subject matter covered. It is sold with the understanding
that the publisher is not engaged in rendering legal, accounting, or other
professional advice. If legal advice or other expert assistance is required, the
services of a competent professional should be sought. The opinions expressed
by the author in this book are not endorsed by Best Seller Publishing®
and are the sole responsibility of the author rendering the opinion.

For more information, please write:
Best Seller Publishing®
1775 US-1 #1070
St. Augustine, FL 32084
or call 1 (626) 765-9750
Visit us online at: www.BestSellerPublishing.org

CONTENTS

FOREWORD

by

Jennifer Bortman

Thank you, my love, for allowing me the opportunity to introduce you in your very first book. Now that you've started writing, I have a feeling this will lead to many other awesome experiences. I promise to always support you, love you unconditionally, and of course challenge you to your highest potential.

A Monumental Move
(A Glimpse into My Oleg's Life)

Like in many immigrant families, Oleg's childhood was one of very humble beginnings. His mother (known as Baba to many) did whatever it took to put food on the table and keep a roof over her family's head. A very sharp woman, she shaped Oleg into the man he is today.

Oleg's father, Deda (God rest his soul), was the epitome of your old school Eastern European father. He was very tough on his family while being very protective. While Deda was not perfect, he loved his family and had the willpower of 100 men.

At a very young age, Deda ran away from home (we believe when he was only eight years old), already drinking vodka, smoking, getting into trouble, and narrowly surviving some near-death experiences. Somehow, fate brought Baba and Deda together, and they were married by 1969. After being married and having children, Baba knew she wanted more for her family.

In 1979, Baba and Deda decided to make the trek to the United States, with the sponsorship of the Jewish Community Center. Oleg was only three years old and his sister, Marina, was six years old. While I always knew this was a monumental move for their family, now that I am a mom, I certainly have a greater respect and admiration for Oleg's parents. They came to this country to escape persecution and to one day have their kids live the American Dream.

The American Dream may have different connotations for each and every one of us. Today, for our family, living the American Dream is very simple — the key ingredient is working hard! Oleg's family worked hard to achieve their success and prosperity.

Over the years, people have said that we shouldn't stereotype his family. Instead of getting defensive, I ask two simple questions:

1.   Why is it bad to live the American Dream?
2.   Why is it bad to point out stereotypes?

If you too are of this mindset, I encourage you to research the essence of the American Dream, and even stereotypes, to create an informed opinion. Maybe you are living the American Dream, you know someone who is, or you are now looking at it from a different point of view. The purpose of Oleg creating this book of stories of a series of accomplished leaders is to share with you that — whether you are from Europe, living on the streets, striving as a single mom, or anything in between — you too can live the American Dream.

Always Love and Adoration

I am proud to say, my 100 percent Jewish Eastern European husband (according to DNA testing) is living the American Dream. It may sound cliché, but he is! His early years of life were not easy by any means. He can elaborate on those chapters of his life if he wants to open up, but I can tell you they were rough.

To put it simply, his parents came over to America with no money, no friends, no family, and not speaking the language. While the first few years were difficult, Oleg was always loved and adored. The way their family shows their love was certainly different from my upbringing. Oleg has told me stories over the years.

Even his adoring mom would plug her nose when watching seven-year-old Oleg play soccer because she thought he was stinking on the soccer field. Then you had his dad. The other soccer parents had no idea what he was screaming in Russian, but I'm sure they were scared and intimidated. While that form of tough love might make some kids cry, it fueled Oleg to continue to play harder and smarter and to practice more. You will find out that this was transferable on and off the soccer field.

That mentality of tough love — two hardworking and devoted parents who wanted Oleg to better his life — fueled the fundamentals and paved the way for him to be the man he is today. Oleg was the first one in his immediate family to graduate with a four-year college degree. His parents were hoping that he would become a doctor or a lawyer. While he considered going into medicine, that was not his calling.

He was extremely successful working in the corporate world. However, he and I both knew that he had the entrepreneurial spirit. To this day, Oleg has an unbelievable talent to not just sell things but do so in a way that is so much more. He is always well informed and confident, and he advocates for what is right.

In 2009, Oleg got his real estate license. At first, he was only doing transactions for our family or friends of the family. His passion for real estate and his ability to provide excellence — in an industry that has a lot of turnover — is what fueled the beginning of his wonderful real estate career. Shortly after getting his license,

Oleg met his soon-to-be business partner, Tucker. The way the two of them fell into each other's lives proves that anything is possible when you keep an open mind.

It all happened with Oleg's first "big" listing. It was my mom's best friend, Dennis, who was selling his home in Phoenix, Arizona. Tucker jokingly started stalking Oleg during his open houses because Tucker wanted the home for himself and his fiancée, Ashley (they too are happily married). That was the start of it all. While Tucker and Oleg have very different personalities, their core values, industry knowledge, and commitment to each other is why I labeled them, rightfully so, as work-soulmates.

That's right, Oleg is living the American Dream and has his work-soulmate. You might ask, what about his personal life? To me, having the balance of work and life is living the dream, and I am happy to share that Oleg and I have been happily married since September 1, 2006. We too met under unique circumstances, and many say we should write a book or movie on that alone. In 2002, we met in the customs line in the Cayman Islands. I was 18 years old and had just finished my first year of college at Northern Arizona University (NAU). Oleg was 26 years old, already living the life of a successful Jersey businessman.

To say the least, Oleg and I were living two very different lives, but there was something special about our first interactions with each other. My mom even called it while we were on the trip — her words, almost exactly, were, "One day that boy is going to want to marry you." At the time, I didn't even think Oleg liked me, but moms are always right! We remained distant friends for a few years because he lived back East and I was still in college.

When Oleg said he was moving out West … well, the rest is history. We started dating in the beginning of, and became engaged at the end of, 2005 — and married in September of 2006. When you know, you know! Oleg's point was, If we know, then why wait?! So yes, Oleg is my soulmate, best friend, and the father of our two amazing babies (10 and 12 years old at the time of this writing). He has not only created this amazing life for himself but has also impacted and influenced my life in so many ways.

He is an amazing communicator and looks at life with such a unique perspective. He loves to coach — even when he doesn't realize he is coaching — and many times coaches when he isn't even asked. He has the ability to not dwell on situations from the past and really have a forward-looking approach to life.

By no means is Oleg perfect. But he does remind me that if we only have a few arguments a year out of 365 days, we are doing great. When he puts it like that, the grade of a 360/365 is 98.6, which is an A+ in my book. And who doesn't love earning an A+! In fact, many years ago, we made a pact that we are always ahead!

We will continue to live by our family mantra:

> Yesterday was the past.
> Tomorrow is the future.
> Today is the present,
> a true gift from God.

Oleg — I am so proud of your past accomplishments, and I will always believe in your dreams.

INTRODUCTION

My name is Oleg Bortman, and I am the most optimistic person you'll ever meet. Most optimistic people believe the glass is half full. I have coined the phrase "My glass is always full." And why do I say that? Well, once you know where I come from — or if you ever meet my mom — I think you will understand why I feel I'm the most blessed person on this planet.

I was born in 1975 to a Jewish immigrant family in Ukraine, which was at that time part of the Soviet Union. We came over to the United States in August of 1979. The timing is significant because the U.S. closed its borders in 1980, blocking any immigration from the Soviet Union for almost eight years. We missed that by less than a year!

When we moved to the states, my mom was thirty, my father was forty-two, my sister was six, and I was about three and a half years old. We were sponsored by a family at the Jewish Community Center in New Jersey. And that's what we started calling home. As we were Jewish immigrants from the Soviet Union, we didn't speak any English. We spoke only Russian. And on top of learning a new language, my parents had to find entirely new trades.

When I started going to school, as I only understood Russian and couldn't really communicate with other children my age, I was ridiculed and teased quite a bit. As we adjusted to our new home, my mom was the biggest optimist. Her theory and her beliefs in life always amounted to "When one door closes, the next door that opens is going to be twice as big." And my father, a super hard worker, was our example of work ethic, integrity, and how your word is your bond. That's how I was raised.

Like many Jewish kids, I grew up playing chess. I enjoyed sports as well. As many Russian or Ukrainian kids do, I grew up playing soccer. And in our house, second place was first loser. So I made sure I overworked myself, practicing harder than I did the day before. I didn't compare myself to other people. I was always comparing myself to how I played the day before or the week before.

While I was going through school, I wanted to become a professional soccer player. However, my parents, like in any other Jewish family, wanted their kids to be either doctors or lawyers. So, in accordance with their wishes for me to become a doctor, I went down that path, earning a degree in bio premed.

After graduating from college, I took a job with a pharmaceutical company, working in a lab as a molecular biologist for about two years. My parents thought I should start taking steps toward taking my MCAT — or that I should try one more career. I chose the latter, and at 23, I found a job at another pharmaceutical company, Abbott Laboratories. This time, I was working as a sales rep — which changed my whole life and perspective.

Abbott Labs was one of the most prestigious postgraduate employers. Like all other large pharmaceutical companies, they invest a lot in their talent. I had an incredible mentor, Mary Gullo, who looked out for me for the first half of my career at Abbott Labs. She taught me many things about business acumen. She taught me how to manage, how to work with people, and also how to develop them.

While I would adjust my vision every two or three years, I was getting promoted, winning sales trips, and I was in the President's Club — the top 10 percent of the sales team. Year after year, it continued to be an awesome job. And I call it a "job" very intentionally. In your life, you'll find things that you like to do that are jobs — and then ultimately, at one of your quarters in your life, you will find a career. Your career will make you happy for the rest of your life.

At some point, I received an important book. I was never a big reader, but it really intrigued me: *Rich Dad Poor Dad* by Robert Kiyosaki. While it covers real estate, it's really about so much more. Kiyosaki shared a concept that stuck with me from day one, and it is affirmed in my life every day. He explained how there are two ways to be valued in life:

1. You're working for your money, meaning you get a job. Someone tells you you're worth $100K, so you're worth $100K. And over time, you'll get promotions and get a raise, increasing by various percentages. Maybe you even get a job making a million dollars a year, followed by raises and bonuses.
2. Your money works for you.

That kind of intrigued me. I didn't understand that concept for a long time.

I continued reading the book, which explained how Kiyosaki's dad, an immigrant, worked very hard in his blue collar job. Meanwhile, Kiyosaki had a best friend whose dad was a university tenured professor. In terms of retirement, the professor was making $75K a year and would have a big lump sum of money in his pension and 401(k). Meanwhile, Kiyosaki's father at some point started investing in real estate and was acquiring properties. In the end, his net worth was larger than that of somebody who went to high school and college and earned a PhD to become a professor. This story really resonated with me, as a Jewish immigrant growing up in America — in a house where second place meant being the first loser.

After reading *Rich Dad Poor Dad*, I continued working harder and smarter. Halfway through my career at Abbott, I had been promoted several times. My next promotion involved me relocating from New Jersey to Las Vegas, where I would be a district and regional manager. In Vegas, I had the pleasure of working for another great, inspirational human being, Jeremy Schubert. (You will learn from him in Chapter 7.)

As I was moving up at the company, I was running into and finding more mentors who would challenge the status quo. There were people who drank the Kool-Aid, who were practically always saying, "Abbott's the best, Abbott's the best" — and I was one of them. I loved the culture. I loved the opportunities they gave me. But I was also always curious about how things worked in life, and why.

I remember in school, I received a report card with a note that said, "Ollie always asks the most questions in class." My mom kept all my report cards — you can ask my wife. I may not have found a lot of achievement as a young student, but since that young age, I have always been curious. I've wanted to know how everything works. Over the course of my childhood, I learned that I didn't need to reinvent the wheel and that I didn't want to experience challenges or losses that other people have. Because of this, I've been able to find shortcuts to winning by living through other people's experiences that they share with me through mentorship.

Life in Four Quarters

This brings me to the intention behind my book. Mentorship continues to be a high value aspect of living. People have invested in me throughout my life, and I'm forever thankful. Part of my inspiration in writing is passing this forward to others. But before I share what happened next in my journey, the end of my time at Abbott and beyond, let's take a moment to address the structure.

Similar to certain sports, I see life operating in four quarters —
followed by overtime (OT). I grew up in sports. I played soccer,
where we had two halves. But like most kids, I also grew up watching
basketball and football. They both intrigued me when I was younger,
but I never excelled at either. I did, however, enjoy running around
— anything that involved chasing a ball and playing with friends on
a team. Nevertheless, I think working with four main stages better
illustrates many of our experiences, and I'm hoping it creates a
realistic breakdown for which you can navigate and identify.

Quarter #1

This stage covers life from birth until around the age of 21 (depending on your situation). This is really the educational stage of your
early existence. So, according to the "standard" path, you're born,
you go to pre-K, kindergarten, elementary school, middle school,
high school, and then to college for your first degree. Obviously,
this can play out in many different ways, you might receive your
education from alternative sources, and maybe your first quarter
ends at a later age.

Quarter #2

This is the stage when you're taking your educational experience out
into the real world, So, for the purposes of this book, this probably
covers ages 21 to 40. If you've completed your education, then this
is your first postgraduate job. Most adults will have a few career
changes or hate a number of jobs before they find their true calling.
During this time, I think most adults will change jobs or careers
three to five times. With the right mentor (I recommend finding at
least three to five mentors), and by investing in yourself correctly,
you will find your true calling later.

During Quarter #2 was when I found my calling at Abbott. I started making some nice money in the late '90s, and I read *Rich Dad Poor Dad*. It really intrigued me, and I was suddenly beginning to see the difference between working for my money and having my money work for me. And that really got me started on asking more and more of the right questions. This shift in mindset is why I had about three or four career changes between the ages of 21 and 40.

Quarter #3

At the time of this writing, this is where I am! This stage often occurs with people between the ages of 41 and about 55. This is after halftime. You're coming back onto the court or the field. You've had a chance to get in touch with your coach in order to evaluate how you and your team did in the first two quarters. You're motivated. You're all pumped up. Hopefully you can take the time to evaluate yourself after your various changes in career.

Now you're ready for the prime years of growing your career and your financial wealth. Why do I say that? Because you've already learned at school, where academia teaches you structure and promptness. It doesn't really teach a lot about the real world. So, between the ages of 21 and 40, you test your education in the real world. You may change careers three to five times. Along the way, you may pick up four or five mentors and really value what you learn from them. So now you have the combined background of academia as well as up to 20 years of work experience.

In Quarter #3, you put it all together for prime wealth, growth time, and working in a career you truly love. When you love what you do, you do it at a higher level than just showing up to work every day. So this is a time that you wake up every day, you go to work, and you don't call it work.

As inspired by Kiyosaki, my true calling was real estate. I got my real estate license in my mid-30s. Today I am a co-founder and co-owner of a real estate brokerage here in Phoenix, Arizona. And I absolutely love what I do every single day. I've been doing this now for over 12 years.

During my third quarter, my business partner and I started our company. We began as just being a team in real estate generating $1 million a year. When we were selling over $25 million, we bought a broker out when their company was selling about $35 million. In 2021, our expanded company sold over $350 million — and we reached this point of profit in just five years.

This is when I hit my stride. I found my career, my true calling, and I absolutely love what I do. I also love to coach and mentor other agents in all aspects of business to help them grow their generational wealth. With that in mind, I want you to see your third quarter (between 41 and 55) as the stage where you find your career, your true calling. This is when you're going to elevate all your life experiences, all your book readings into a whole different chapter of your life.

Quarter #4

At this stage, it's showtime. There are 12 minutes left in a basketball game. In your fourth quarter, you're between the ages of 55 and 70. If you've already had a family, you may now be reaching the point where you and your spouse are empty nesters. If so, maybe you and your life partner are starting to travel — even if it's to visit your children at their college campuses or their new homes. If you never had kids, then you certainly might be raising pets, like cats or dogs — which are kind of like four-legged kids.

Nevertheless, you've been following your true calling. In this quarter, you're using the wealth that you have accrued to really experience and start living life. You're in that final push of your career. You're probably getting tired, so this is when you're starting to take time off and vacation. Maybe you're traveling or finally dedicating time to personal experiences. Everyone typically has a bucket list, and this is the final stage for accruing enough financially to get those items tallied off after retirement.

Overtime (OT)

Depending on your plans, lifestyle, and finances, you're probably retiring between 65 and 70. At this point, you're not working anymore. You're finding more hobbies, more interests, more friends, and you're living the last stage of your life.

The one thing none of us know, and none of us can predict, is the day that we will die. So it's important to figure out what you're leaving behind. This stage is all about legacy and reaching the end of your journey on your terms. In terms of legacy, this is also when you're finding more opportunities to invest in others as a mentor — directly interacting with individuals in their first or second quarters — or as a philanthropist — donating your time and resources to greater causes and people in need.

As I'm about to share, part of the inspiration behind my book plays into this for me. Because of how my third quarter is playing out, I can get started a little early on my legacy.

The Gift of the Present

As shared at the beginning of this introduction, my mantra is "My glass is always full." Now I'd like to share a prayer that I say to my kids every night: "Yesterday was the past. Tomorrow's the future. Today is the present, a true gift from God."

It doesn't matter whether you're religious or spiritual. As a math or science person, or a believer in the divine, one thing we do know is that the only guarantees in life are death and taxes. So, just as we have no idea when the next generation begins or the next person will be born, you have no idea when your time is up on this planet. Tomorrow is never guaranteed.

Just as I pray with my kids, I live every day as if it is a "present," and a gift from God. Every day I wake up is a blessing in which I have an opportunity to positively impact my life — or, more importantly, impact somebody else's life.

Again, I was born in a communist country, the Soviet Union, in 1975. We came to the United States as Jewish immigrants. And we live in the best country in the world. Here, our people fight for freedoms. Our first responders on the streets protect our freedoms every day. Unless you were born in circumstances similar to mine or those of other immigrants who risked their lives to change their whole trajectory by leaving home, like my family did, you may still take this for granted. I hope you can understand how lucky or blessed we are for presents we receive every day, just being here in America.

I want to carry that blessing forward. So, in this book, you're going to hear from a dozen people who impacted my life and who have also changed their trajectory. They are fellow business entrepreneurs — very successful people from different backgrounds and facets of life. The reason I incorporated so many different special people is because part of my intention with this book is to help others understand there is more than one way to be successful in America. This is one of the only countries I know of where you can be a millionaire today, broke two days later, and then a week later be a millionaire again. In communist and various socialist countries, you don't have those growth opportunities, ever.

So, for all the readers out there, you'll see professionals of different life paths who are examples of why America is the best place. I believe we need to protect that aspect of our country. It should always remain a home that gives every person the right to freedom and success — whether they were born here or not. The United States is the only country that provides so many opportunities, and

I hope to illustrate this with the variety of contributing authors I was able to gather for you.

No matter where you're born, no matter where you're from, no matter what your background is — there will always be somebody who will invest in or trust in you. As I or any author in this book mentions anything about investing in ourselves or others, I want to ensure you understand what we mean. This book is not necessarily about investing in the traditional sense — like acquiring a house, stock, crypto, property, or art for an ROI or REIT. These authors are investors who invested in their own education and experience during their first two quarters — and who were themselves investees, guided by important mentors along the way.

The chapters included are intended to be an investment in who you are as a human being. So the journey's ahead of you, and I hope this prospective investment will open up your eyes. Also, the journey of investing in this book will show you how you can invest in yourself and the sort of people you can receive investments from throughout your four quarters.

Throughout my childhood, my mom would always encourage me to believe in myself. So I grew up believing in myself. And overall, by the end of this book, I hope you'll see you should not only believe in yourself — you should definitely invest in yourself as well.

1ST QUARTER

After my family moved from the Soviet Union to the United States as Jewish immigrants, my sister and I were their number one assets. I know this to be true because they sacrificed everything to bring us to the land of opportunity. They also sacrificed even more to secure work in order to give us the life they dreamed of providing us with.

When we arrived in New Jersey, we were supported by the Jewish Community Center. Over the course of my childhood, we received education through schools and teachers. There were mentors, counselors, coaches, and employers along the way who helped us prepare for the real world. In all cases, these investments were made because we were number one assets.

As soon as you are born, your first quarter begins. This is the foundation of the rest of your life. As far as I'm concerned, this stage concludes around the age of 21. Depending on the timing and situations of your life, you will have finished public school along with some form of education — or you're on your way to completing it. While this could be a bachelor's degree, it could also be trade school or some other significant certification.

In the world of sports, this is a crucial part of an athlete's life. Arrangements need to be made for getting involved with coaches and clubs. Training is secured in order to begin creating instincts and skills for peak performance. Through high school, emphasis is placed on attaining scholarships, which will provide great options for college. And through college, emphasis is placed on creating scouting opportunities.

For athletes, an ideal first quarter ends with them entering professional leagues. Along the way, phenomenal figures (usually coaches) share their mindsets, strategies, and methods in order for the athlete — the number one asset — to enter their second quarter on the best possible terms. This plays out a little differently for the rest of us.

The environment you were raised in will ultimately make you a great person in society. During this quarter, you are a huge sponge. The main resources or nutrients are absorbed from your parents (or guardians), teachers, coaches, tutors, elders, and friends. The leaders in your life are investing in you, because you are a number one asset.

I know for some of you, it doesn't feel that way. Ideally, you have parents and a community who love and nourish you. At the very least, you have teachers in your life who want to prepare you for the real world. These adults are investing in you. Of course, there's the literal idea of this. There is the financial cost of food, water, shelter, and education. But there is also the investment of wisdom, knowledge, and emotional support.

This investment is provided because you are a number one asset. I need you to believe this about yourself. Just as you were invested in, you need to continue investing in yourself. Hopefully, by the time you finish your first quarter, you are at least beginning to see yourself in this light.

So, let's get started.

ABOUT RANDY TIPTON

 Born in Brooklyn, New York, Randy Tipton grew up with a father who was a kosher butcher who worked six days a week — as well as long hours. Randy loved the time they were able to have together. Over the years, she would hear her father discourage his children from following in his footsteps. He wanted them to join the professional world. Randy accomplished this by starting as a file clerk at an insurance company and creating a career that now spans 50 years. She is a proud business owner who has dedicated herself to an industry that she loves.

Randy is particularly proud that her daughter followed in her footsteps and will soon take over the role of president of their beautiful company. Randy will continue to work but will step down and allow her daughter's brilliance to shine. This is an amazing time for their business and family!

1

MORE THAN FINE!

by
Randy Tipton

I came from a traditional Jewish family. Hardworking and faithful. We did not have much financially, but that did not matter, as we had each other. I was born in Brooklyn, New York, where my father and my grandfather were kosher butchers. My dad worked six days a week as well as long hours. On Saturdays he and I would go to synagogue together and spend the day with each other. This was the best day for me, to simply be with him.

We lived in an apartment complex in Brooklyn. When I was about five years old, we experienced a fire and lost everything we owned. Months later, my parents moved us to Syracuse, New York, and my dad started over, working for a local kosher butcher. He eventually bought his own shop again but always discouraged us, my brother and me, from following in his footsteps. He wanted us to join the professional world. I accomplished this by starting as a file clerk at an insurance company and creating a career that now spans 50 years.

I am a proud business owner and have dedicated myself to this industry that I love. My son is an extremely successful businessman. And I am particularly proud that my daughter followed in my footsteps and is soon to take over my role as president of our beautiful company. I will continue to work but will step down and allow her brilliance to shine. This is an amazing time for our business and family! The most important aspect of my life and what provides me with the utmost pride is that both of my children are good people, amazing parents, and two of the best human beings I know!

My parents taught me about hard work. When I was a child I was not aware of the sacrifices that they made for my brother and me but came to recognize this as I raised my children. I got married young and did not attend college, and, unfortunately, my marriage was not as successful as my parents' marriage was. So I raised my kids as a single parent. My focus was always on my children. I worked hard and learned on the job, taking classes in the industry that I chose. My hard work and ethical commitment gave me opportunities to get promoted and grow in my field. I also changed employers when necessary to further my career and take care of my children. It was not easy, but it was perfect!

The one story that I would like to share is about the investment that I made, as a single parent, in my two children. My highest priority was to raise my children to be ethically strong, have faith, and be loving and honest and well educated. I made myself a promise that my children would be independent young adults and that I would provide them with a college education so that they could start their adult lives debt-free and ready to face the world!

My days were long, and thank goodness my parents lived nearby to help me with picking up the kids and attending sporting events. There was not much time for me, but I did not really think about that at the time. I worked, then went straight home for homework, activities, dinner, and off to bed!

Days were long. I studied after the kids went to sleep. I was careful to live within our means. Every so often, I spent our extra money — when we had some — on music lessons and athletic activities for the kids. I did not think that I was sacrificing because I was achieving the goal I'd set for myself! The kids flourished with great grades and good friends, and they were respectful and appreciative. I taught them to handle their own money and be debt averse. I spoke with them about my goal for them to be the first people in our family to have college degrees, and they were proud of their accomplishments.

You can imagine my pride as I sat in the audience when my son graduated from Arizona State University and, years later, my daughter graduated from Northern Arizona University! Both of them achieved what I'd dreamed of, and then some.

I believe that this life lesson of thinking of others before yourself, being devoted to your family, working hard, and being honest and ethical has created a foundation for both of my children. And, as a business owner, mentor, and coach, I bring all of these elements to my everyday life. As I reflect on myself as a young parent with two children and no college education, I realize now how "scrappy" I was. At the time, I just did what was needed, but now I see how my inner strength and character led me to who I am today.

My salary, when the kids were young, was not very much. I had a mortgage to pay and needed to focus on having healthy food on the table and providing the children with extracurricular activities and a good life. We lived in an upscale neighborhood, and there was pressure for them to dress the way other kids did and attend events and summer vacations that were well beyond my means.

Being financially responsible was a saving grace for me — as well as continuing to better myself for the good of my family. This was back in the day when there was little to no flexibility regarding hours worked. I had a 45-minute drive to work each way, and every day, I worked a full eight-hour day. And, as I said earlier, it was after the kids went to bed that I worked on extra projects and studied to obtain more knowledge and expertise. I did all of this, knowing, believing, and recognizing that I would fulfill my dream!

Inevitable Challenges

There were setbacks. The teenage years added a new dimension of worry and concern. I kept all of this to myself as I did not want to burden my parents with problems that I was solving. This led me to a long period of time when the phrase "I am fine" was what I said each and every day — even on days when I was not fine! I learned to be stoic. To solve serious problems. And to always keep my focus on my vision!

I also, unfortunately, inherited some physical ailments that created a lot of pain and discomfort for me. This was difficult for me to accept because I needed to be strong and healthy for everyone. However, the pain increased, and I was facing surgeries and more painful complications. I woke up every morning and put on my "happy face," not wanting anyone to know how much pain I was in.

I learned that being stoic and always "being fine" was good but created some holes in my life. I did not allow people — friends or family — to help me. I thought that I had to do everything myself. While being independent is a good and strong character trait, I brought it to a new level; I became increasingly aware of this as my children became such amazing and responsible adults. Not only were they able to help me, they wanted to help me — and I had to learn to accept this as an act of love and respect toward them.

It is truly an act of love to allow others to help you. It makes your loved ones feel good and respected. And after much resistance on my side, I recognized this as an act of giving to my family. To allow them to do for me what I had done for them.

I accomplished my promise through hard work, setting a good example, and remaining focused on my number one priority — my family. This was not easy, as I was working and often had to sacrifice to provide for them. However, I did not consider it a sacrifice — instead I considered this chapter in my life an investment in my family and the love of my children.

There was a point in my life when putting on my happy face became more and more difficult. The kids were grown and knew that I was struggling, but I told everyone "I am fine." My usual smile was still on my face, but I felt that it was plastered there. I journaled about my passage. It brought me back to my goal as a young woman to raise my children to be ethically strong, have faith, and be loving and honest and well educated. I accomplished this goal and now had to give them the opportunity to give back. To help me. This was actually a gift of love from me to them. Once I recognized this and opened up and asked for help, the burden was shifted. It was shared. It was accepted with love and gratitude.

More Than Fine

This past year has been particularly difficult. I am months away from turning 70 and have a burning desire to continue to be youthful, present, and an integral part of my kids' and grandkids' lives. However, I have been struggling with some botched surgeries and have just not been feeling well.

I again opened up to my family, sharing my feelings, my concerns and even fear. I have also learned to talk about my concerns to my closest friends, and the outpouring of love and support gives me buoyancy and feelings of hope. I reflected on my strength in raising my children and decided to use my powers to improve my health! And this is the path that I am on — with the love, support, and friendship of so many who love me and want to help me.

Finally, after almost 70 years of taking care of others, I am focused on taking care of myself. AND, most importantly, I am not alone. The investment that I made in my family has paid off. I am pleased to say that my health is improving, I am so positive and energetic about the future and my family, and we are closer than we have ever been.

Life is a daily lesson. What did I learn today? And what is on the horizon for tomorrow? I suggest taking every day as an opportunity to learn. To grow. And to improve someone's life. Sometimes it is helping others, and sometimes it is helping yourself. Always have confidence and know that you can achieve your goals!

ABOUT JASON KUSH

 Owner of J. P. Kush Construction, LLC, Jason Kush's company was founded on one central belief: Your home should be as unique and individual as you are. That's why they created the Your Home, Your Way semi-customization model. Homeowners have the ability to take already highly upgraded base models and make selections and customizations that make the home uniquely theirs.

Serving Scottsdale and Phoenix, Arizona, as well as the rest of the Valley of the Sun since 2008, Jason Kush welcomes you to J. P. Kush Construction. Having been raised in the valley as a second-generation developer, he is a licensed residential and commercial general contractor, as well as a licensed real estate broker.

Kush has seen this valley change a great deal in 40 years, and he's been involved in many of those changes! He is also an alumni of the W. P. Carey School of Business at Arizona State, with a B.S. in Marketing as well as numerous years of Sales Management experience from two Fortune 10 companies. His insights, background, and skills allow him to have a very different and unique perspective from that of his peers. Welcome home to J. P. Kush Construction, LLC.

2

BUILDING CHARACTER

by
Jason Kush

There are a million and one business books and self-help books with catch phrases and pearls of wisdom out there. And you know what? Each of them makes a valid point and has something you can learn from them. I personally like "It takes 10,000 hours to become an expert at something." It's true!

The question really isn't about what advice you need. The question is what advice do you need based upon your story. Your story is what makes you uniquely you. And your story usually comes from that place of *what doesn't kill you makes you stronger!* Your story is about those experiences and those million choices you made to make, well, you!

It's all about character building. I believe that all successful people have one very strong and similar trait ... they have a strong character. That may be a good or bad character. But it is a character not only unique to them but unique to the world. They are that person you see and say, "They are true to themselves. They are true to their beliefs. They are true to their goals." Being that true to oneself is in itself a unique characteristic.

My character was molded very early on, starting in a way similar to many children of divorce. I can remember the day my dad left like it was yesterday. I was 11 years old and in the back end of fifth grade. It was a super dark and stormy evening, with the rain coming down so hard that you could not only hear the runoff from the roof, you could hear it pounding on the roof louder than our tears could drown it out. My brother and I were standing at the door with my mother as my father was standing on the front porch, leaving our family. Like something out of a movie. At least, that's how my mind created the memory.

In hindsight, that was the day that changed my life forever. Up to that moment, from my and the outside world's view, we had a perfect little family in the middle of the '80s. My father was a rising star in the Arizona building and construction world. My mother was a homemaker like one out of a 1950s sitcom.

We all had great close friends, and our childhood was without care or worry. We rode our bikes to school. And as soon as we got home, we left again on those bikes with our friends. Our families had a general idea of where we were. We all just knew when the streetlights came on, it was time to head home for dinner. We had Ataris to keep us entertained. Phones were connected to the wall via a very long cord, and cable television was relatively new. All we knew was that life seemed great, we had no real struggles, and we were all happy.

However, over the course of a few months, my life went into a tailspin, and I had to grow up really fast!

As the school year finished, my mother moved with me and my brother to California to be near her family. Normally, this would be totally understandable. However, my mother had failed beforehand to mention this move to my father, my Arizona family members, and my brother and me. The only remaining stable things, our home and friends, were now being ripped out from under us too.

So there I was, in California now … a sad, depressed child with no friends and a mother who kept him in the dark. Unfortunately, that same mother was going to make my life a living hell. You see, it turns out, I was way too similar to my father. And my mother was entirely heartbroken and angry with him. That anger was unleashed upon me in the form of physical abuse. Not only did that abuse happen as over-the-top punishment when she felt it was warranted … it was unleashed upon me every time I behaved like or discussed my father. This abuse became routine, consistent over the next three and a half years.

Skill Sets of Character

Where others see sadness and regret, I see the period that formed the foundation of who I was. These lessons have stuck with me my entire life — lessons that helped me search for what I needed to build my character.

#1: COURAGE

When faced with destruction all around you, the first thing you must do is find your courage. It is always easier to crawl into a proverbial hole or bottle. It takes true inner strength and courage to fight the trials and tribulations in our lives. Some of us have easier trials than others, but we all have rough spots in our lives. When those times come, we must have internal courage to rise up and face those challenges. No one can make you do anything in this life — your actions are 100 percent up to you!

#2: STRENGTH

It's one thing to have the internal courage to do something. It is a completely different ability to use that courage and do something with it. That ability lies completely in your inner strength. Not only does that give you the ability to get started, but it maintains you throughout the journey. Strength is a mental ability that you must work on personally every day. If you can't, this is an area for which a professional therapist or counselor would be a valuable resource.

#3: DRIVE

You had the courage to make a change and have the strength to execute it. You need the drive to maintain yourself to seeing your ideas, your dreams, and your aspirations fulfilled. Drive is something that also can renew itself every day. You need to wake up every morning and decide what you are going to accomplish that day. Then, at the end of that day, reflect upon what was and wasn't accomplished, and why.

I use my calendar by blocking out periods of time to get specific tasks done. For example, this chapter had small blocks of time set aside over several weeks to accomplish this goal.

#4: FRIENDS/FAMILY

You have heard the saying "It takes a village" (more on this from Stuart M. Crawford in Chapter 6). It's another true pearl of wisdom! If COVID taught us anything, it showed us how interconnected we are and how much we need one another. In my case, my family was the one thing I couldn't depend on. I had to go out and build a family of my own. I have now done that twice in my life.

My first family is my closest group of high school friends. The five of us are lovingly known as "the Idiots" and are brothers who speak daily and have for 33-plus years now.

The other is the family I have built with my amazing wife, Jennifer, and our three children. The four of them are my why. They are why I get up every day and do what I do.

#5: PASSION

You need to have a reason to get up every day and do what you do. That's your passion. You do not want to live to work. You want to work to live. You want to create the resources of time and money so that you can do the things that make life worth living.

For me, it's travel. We live in a truly remarkable and diverse world. I want my family to see as much of it as we can with the time that we have on this planet.

Building Your Character

Building character to me really is about developing the above five skill sets. You develop and grow these skill sets through your journey. For my personal journey, I decided that as a young person, I was no longer going to be a victim and that I was going to take control of my situation. I started that by standing up to my mother. Yes, that did make things worse …

But it gave me courage.

That courage helped me develop an inner strength. A strength and determination that I never knew I had. Once I started to make changes for the positive in my life, it awoke in me a drive that had never been there. It was a drive that told me not only that I needed to get out of that horrible situation, but I also wanted to make something special of my life. This is a drive that still is going strong to this day.

That drive made me want to build a new family to help support me. A family of friends of my own creation. I was able to gather people around me who not only cared about me but also made me a better person. The "birds of a feather flock together" expression holds true. You need to surround yourself with people who you want to be like, or who are like you (if you are the person you want to be).

In my case, these friends also helped me get out of my precarious situation. They helped me get back to Arizona, away from that abusive situation. And they helped set me on a trajectory for success as a second generation developer.

I also used my drive to better the community I live in. For me, it's all about kids and the arts. For years I was a member of the Phoenix 20/30 club. Not only did I make lifelong friends, but that club also allowed me to help and give back to underprivileged youth. Like me, they were dealing with things they shouldn't have needed to deal with during their childhood.

I also became very involved with the arts. The arts is how humanity leaves its mark on the world. It's our way of communicating our joys and struggles with one another. It's our way of communicating what it's like to be human.

That singular act of leaving my mother and California and returning to Arizona helped me find my passion. I had always enjoyed my creative side, but it was never a driving force for me. Spending hours upon hours on job sites in my youth allowed me to realize that creativity could be used in home building.

I truly love and will forever be passionate about the homes I build and the neighborhoods I develop. I respect the fact that these houses become someone's home — the place where they live their lives and create those memories that make life worth living. And yes, for all of those Freudian psychoanalysts out there … I am sure, deep down, I am trying to create the perfect home for my clients since that's something I didn't have as a child. Maybe that's just my way of trying to make the world a little better than I found it.

So, in your journey of building your character, use those business and personal self-help books that speak to you and will fill that spot in making you a better you!

ABOUT CALEB SPEARS

 By the age of 24, Caleb Spears had already generated over $2 million in gross commissions selling luxury real estate along Florida's Emerald Coast. From a young age, Caleb's passion about people and how interpersonal relationships relate to business was evident. Caleb spent his formative years feverishly studying books, listening to podcasts, and absorbing any piece of wisdom he could find regarding the skill of leadership.

At the age of 18, he got his Florida real estate license and, along with his older brother Jonathan, co-founded the Spears Group. Spears Group has been consistently ranked by the *Wall Street Journal* as the top team in Northwest Florida by sales volume and has been nominated for awards such as the Inman Top Innovators Award in 2022.

Today, Caleb is not only a top producer in the market, he is also the Director of Agent Development and Training at Spears Group, where he helps grow the businesses of their team that includes both brand-new agents and seasoned veterans who produce $50 million or more in annual sales.

3

WISDOM UNDER PRESSURE

by
Caleb Spears

When I turned 17, my dad decided it was time I got a "real job." My dad is a builder, and I had worked for him during the summers cleaning his job sites, and also on a surveying crew. These jobs were hard in some ways; they were both physically demanding and always took place under the searing heat of the Florida sun. But I didn't have to work any set hours, and it was always working for family friends in a "wink-wink, nudge-nudge, we'll pay you some cash under the table" kind of agreement.

These jobs offered no real pressure and minimal responsibility. I viewed them as an easy way to make a couple hundred dollars, which was endless money as a teenager. But my dad knew something I didn't:

I needed to grow. And pressure makes diamonds.

I protested a bit when my dad initially suggested I go out and start applying for jobs. After all, I had a good life, and I enjoyed my daily ritual of relaxing and playing video games after school. But my dad's stern tone and steely expression made it clear he wasn't just asking.

So, I began applying for work everywhere I could think of. I applied to Starbucks, Bonefish Grill, Chipotle, and even a local diner called The Donut Hole. In total, I applied to over 15 local businesses. During the entire process, I kept praying, "Lord please put me wherever is best for me."

After application number ten got turned down, I started to get discouraged. I figured all I had to do was show up sober to some of these interviews to get hired. On a whim, I dropped an application in at the local Chick-fil-A because they had a "We're hiring" placard next to the cash register. Several months went by while I continued to not hear back from any of the businesses in question. I even had one restaurant tell me, "We want you, when can you start?" but after giving them my availability, they never reached out again.

One day, I glanced at my phone in an airport. I saw that I had a missed call during my flight. The unknown number left me a voice-mail message: "Hey, this is Rick, and I'm opening a new Chick-fil-A in the area. I got your application from the other Chick-fil-A store, and I'd love for you to come in for an interview."

Immediately, I felt a sense of dread. I prayed in my head, "Please Lord. Not Chick-fil-A. Anywhere but there. I don't want to be the cliché Christian kid who works at Chick-fil-A." But I went to the interview because I was getting pretty desperate, and my dad wasn't too pleased that I had yet to find a job.

The interview went just like all the others. I met with the manager, Mohammed, in a small metal trailer (the makeshift leadership team headquarters until construction was completed). I filled out some paperwork and answered some basic questions. Mohammed said, in a courteous but bored tone, "Thanks; we'll let you know if you got the job."

Thank goodness, I thought. I'd heard that before, and I knew where this was headed — another "no" to add to my growing tally. As I got up to leave, Rick walked in and said, "No, no, no, we want you. You're hired!"

I faked a smile and did my best "Wow! Thank you …" with the enthusiasm of a six-year-old who just got underwear for Christmas. It's funny how life works. That job I never wanted was one of the best things to ever happen to me, and I was about to learn one of the best lessons of my life a few short weeks after that fateful day.

Stop Barking …

"Hey, just so you know, everybody here is going to hate you in about two weeks." Mohammed's words came as a shock considering I'd started the job a few days earlier. How could I have managed to do much of anything remarkable during that time, let alone something so horrible?

Mohammed, who was now officially my manager, was kind enough to pull me aside to have this conversation in private.

I managed to breathe the words out, "Mo, what in the world did I do?" despite the mass migration of butterflies that had just found their home in the pit of my stomach.

"The way you speak to people has to change, Caleb. You're running around barking orders at people! You say things like, 'Go get cups! We need more sauces!' as if people are your servants just waiting to be given orders. I understand this is a high-stress environment, and what you're saying isn't exactly wrong. We did need cups. We did need sauces. The needs you're seeing are valid, but the way you communicate them lacks respect for the person you're talking to."

Mo paused for a moment as the weight of his words rested heavy on my shoulders. Seeing the vague sense of confusion and fear in my eyes, he continued: "Instead of giving people orders, try wording things differently. When there's a job you know has to be done, say, 'Hey, Mo! Could you do me a favor? I have to go get sauces, but we're also out of cups. Would you mind grabbing some for us? It would be a huge help!' And when there's multiple jobs needing to be done, always take the one that is the hardest, heaviest, dirtiest! That way you're showing respect to the people around you, and in turn, they'll respect you too."

I wasn't entirely sure it would work, but anything was worth a try to avoid being hated at my first real job. The opportunity to try Mo's tactics presented itself sooner than I'd thought when, during the lunch rush that day, we ran out of ice and cups. The ice "buckets" are really more like small barrels. And when they're filled to the top, they weigh about as much as I did when I was eight years old and my clothes were a size called "husky." We needed three buckets.

I went up to a guy named Danny who constantly scowled at me and seemed to have a genuine dislike of me that teetered on the edge of that hatred Mo had mentioned. I delivered Mo's script with as much fake confidence as I could muster:

"Hey, Danny!" I cried enthusiastically, "Would you be able to do me a favor? I have to grab a couple buckets of ice, but we're also out of cups. Would you mind grabbing us a few from the back? It would be such a huge help!"

I braced, waiting for Danny's trademark scowl and accompanying stare that reminded me of Inigo Montoya preparing to get revenge on the man who killed his father. To my great surprise, that scowl immediately melted into an almost relieved smile, and I heard a shockingly bright tone in his voice: "Sure, Caleb! I'd be happy to." And off he went.

Frankly, if my jaw could have been any lower in that moment, it would've been in the basement. I couldn't believe it worked! *Maybe Mo's onto something.* From that day forward, I vowed to change the way I communicated. No matter how stressful the moment, I chose to take those extra few seconds to communicate a need from a place of humility that bestowed respect and dignity on the person I was talking to. I also learned what it means to lead from the front by volunteering to take the hardest job.

Perhaps the Most Important Sum

What happened that day was such a small moment in Mo's life that I doubt he even remembers it happened. To him, it was a few seconds out of a busy day to talk to a naïve teenager. But for me, that moment was an investment he made that transformed me into a better person. The beauty of investing in people is that it offers the most potent form of compound interest in existence.

Mo's choice to invest his time and wisdom in me didn't change only my life; his lessons ripple throughout the lives of every person I interact with. These ripples are like a torch being passed in an infinite relay race. Sometimes the torch gets passed in subtle ways. I hope it gets passed daily when the people I interact with feel cared for and important by my choice of words. I hope that they notice my gratitude for them and my desire to treat them with that same respect and dignity I was treated with when getting corrected by Mo.

Sometimes I get the privilege of passing the torch of his wisdom on in a more direct manner — like when I counsel a friend or share the fire with a perfect stranger who happens to be reading this book. The ripple effect continues in each of your lives as you absorb the lessons and begin applying them during your day. The cycle repeats as you begin to pass the torch down to the generations of people who will come into your life.

We may never truly know the entire sum of the value created when we choose to make a deposit in the bank account of someone else's life. If we could rewind the tape of history, we'd see that every great person and every great discovery started with a moment just like this. Eventually I was unanimously voted into a leadership position at Chick-fil-A and went on to learn so many more invaluable lessons that have served me in my career since. But that first lesson from Mohammed was the foundation for everything.

Mo didn't have to take time out of his day to help me. He could've just decided I was a jerk or a lost cause and let me self-destruct over the course of the next few weeks. But Mo was a great leader, and he chose to take a moment to help someone under his charge who he saw was struggling. In doing so, Mohammed changed my life.

Let's all be a little more like Mo today and take a moment to show love and respect to the people around us and invest back into them. You never know how far your torch will be passed.

2ND QUARTER

This is a very interesting quarter. Investments have been made in your life, because you are a number one asset. By now, you've earned a foundation of knowledge and wisdom, and you're entering the real world. During this stage, you are going to see why you're the number one asset for yourself. If you haven't already, you will find an internship or job that tests and furthers your foundation. This is the official beginning of finding your true calling.

For athletes, this is the start of a path to some of the greatest wealth they will accrue in the next 20 years. Depending on their skill level and their agent, as they step into professional contracts, some of them stand to earn $1 million and others could make over $500 million. Their next stage is ultimately retirement.

For the rest of us, our next stage is stepping into our actual career. Before you enter your third quarter, around age 40, you have likely been through more than a couple jobs in order to find your passion — the work that fulfills you while you accrue wealth for the future. Along the way, you are also meeting mentors who can help you step further into your best self.

The investments of your youth aren't completely finished. Leaders, managers, employers, and colleagues will set examples and may even invest their time and resources in helping you find your path. They do this because you are a number one asset. And at this stage, you probably aren't quite sure what that means for yourself just yet.

As shared in my introduction, I did not find my career straight out of college. I went through a few different jobs. My second post-graduate job at Abbott Laboratories was imperative in my professional journey. As I believe all employers should, they provided many opportunities for both growth and networking. During my time there, I continued seeing how I was a number one asset, and I continued investing in myself. While lab work and sales were not necessarily my true calling, my experiences and connections helped me discover my specialties in management and empowerment.

As you press forward through your second quarter, you learn what you don't want to do — which is the difference between a job and a career. And you'll learn where you excel and what you need in order to further facilitate that. This could mean more certifications. It could mean a master's degree. This is all an investment for your third quarter where your true calling falls into place and you begin building your future.

It's time to believe that you are a number one asset. Your community believed it. Your mentors believe it. And now it's your turn to see it for yourself.

ABOUT JOHN BOHM

 Jon Bohm is a sought-after Personal and Performance Coach, Business Coach, National Speaker, and Trainer. He is currently CEO and President of Driven Associates and Driven Marketing.

After surviving cancer in his 20s, Jon realized that life is too short not to wake up and enjoy every day. Jon realized how much potential to make a positive impact on the lives of his family and others almost died with him. He challenges his clients and audiences to take full advantage of this one chance at life we have.

4

REDEFINING SUCCESS

by
John Bohm

I want to ask you the most important question that has guided my life at all the important and difficult crossroads. This question is simple and not very easy … Who are you?

I really began to wrestle with this question in my early 20s. I had just been diagnosed with terminal cancer a year earlier. Through some strange events, I was able to see Lance Armstrong's doctor who had just discovered the cure for my cancer (mediastinal semi-noma). All of a sudden, I was one of the first people to gain access to Dr. Larry Einhorn's life work. I then found myself miraculously cured and sitting on the deck of my good friend Steve's house. We were sitting there, solving the world's problems like we often did, with a beer in hand. But the world looked very different to me at that point.

I had just wrestled with God and my own mortality, coming to grips with the reality of death that will face us all. I was beginning to take inventory of everything in my life. Like watching the seasons change, I knew the seasons in my life were about to change in a big way. Like most people who sense this deep inside, I was already staying in the wrong season for too long. Maybe everything in my life was about to change — not because of some external circumstances but because of my own newfound desire to maximize, enjoy, thrive, and live my life to the absolute fullest.

What would you do if you had a second chance at life? We all think we are living life to the fullest, but are you? Or, like me, do you know the seasons need to change and you are waiting too long to do it?

Feeling completely lost on the inside, I realized so many things in my life were being done from the primary motives of fear, obligation, or guilt. The problem with that is, after thinking I was going to die and getting a second chance at life, I found myself unwilling to be motivated by any of those things ever again — even in the smallest ways. Which meant no more useless board meetings, conversations, or events I didn't want to be at.

I realized nothing is more important than time. Time is what life is made of, and I couldn't waste it. Everything was going to change; it had to change, or it was going to implode. I decided I couldn't live by the same rules I did in the first part of my life … but I had absolutely no idea where to go.

Who are you? becomes the most important question in times like these, because it will guide you through the dark haze of these crossroads and will absolutely guarantee your success in everything that you do.

It's a difficult question to answer because you can't look outside of yourself or to anyone else for the answer. No one has ever been where you are going before, because nobody has ever been you before. It's an inward journey, a deep dive, and sometimes a painful excavation to get to the answer. And when you find it, it will change absolutely everything.

Who & Why

I've seen a lot of people fail, lose, and even destroy their lives by failing at their dreams, jobs, and relationships; aging out of sports; dealing with health issues; and the list goes on. We can all lose at a lot of different things, but the one thing we can never lose at is being ourselves to the fullest extent possible.

What would happen if you woke up tomorrow and did exactly what you wanted to do? No shoulds. No fear. No obligation. No guilt. Just you in the rawest form, waking up and being you to the fullest extent possible.

So many people wake up and go to a job they don't love, stay in relationships they don't enjoy, or wear clothes and get haircuts they don't like, because they're afraid they won't be accepted or they feel trapped by their jobs, or because of a million other fears or "responsibilities."

What if all of those feelings were gone and you just woke up and did exactly what you wanted? If you were the purest, most authentic and best version of yourself. Would the world accept you? Would your spouse? What would your friends and family think? Would your current job still work?

Does that scare you? It scared me. But for me, after cancer, I was done being scared, and it was time to do what I wanted. After all, if you can fail at all the things you don't want, you might as well try to live the life you do want. But what exactly is that? Of course, the secret is that this is exactly how you guarantee your success.

Have you ever seen someone who doesn't seem to fit the right mold of what you had in your head for success, or a particular job, and they are crushing it? How can this be? How is the lady with the mohawk the most successful person in the room? Don't get me wrong; just because you don't fit the mold doesn't mean you will find success. There are a lot of unauthentic "try-hards" out there. That's not what I'm talking about. I'm talking about guaranteeing success by being the most authentic version of yourself. Defining success in a way that is truly your own version of that word.

My Second Life

It was time for me to define my success, and my then profession as a pastor was no longer going to work. I had to quit. I had to do everything differently. But how?

I needed to build a new life, but I had no blueprint. So, I asked my friend Steve, "What would you do if you could no longer be a teacher? If you had to start over?" He said he would fall back on his woodworking skills and do carpentry things. The problem for me was that I didn't have any tangible skills coming to mind. I wasn't even sure if I could build a birdhouse.

Theology, public speaking, teaching, and helping other people didn't seem like the right skill set to build a life on. Or so I thought. That conversation got the wheels turning: first, *what skills do I have?* But I soon found this line of thought to be a rabbit hole that captured me for the next year.

Tangible skills are on the surface. However, I needed to find out what I wanted. *What do I really want, not just in a career but out of life? Who am I at the deepest levels? What am I motivated by? What do I want to be motivated by? What would I do if no one was looking? If there was no praise or criticism, who would I be? What am I great at? What do I suck at? What has my life story given me? What has my life story taken from me? What do I need to keep? What no longer serves me? What am I uniquely good at? Who do I want to become?*

I had a lot to discover about who I am and who I wanted to be. You can do the same for you.

Start by taking some profiles. There are three of them you can take for free on my website. They take about ten minutes each. See Oleg's online author page. From there, you will have a foundational place to see how you interact with people, jobs, communication, motivational styles, environments, money, aesthetics, learning, and much more. The third profile will give you invaluable insights into your subconscious: how you really view people, planning, productivity, objects, and yourself, even when you don't realize it.

Using the profiles as a guide, start the questions:

1. Who are you? Who do you want to be?
2. Who would you be without praise or criticism? Without the need for money?
3. What are you great at? What are you terrible at?
4. What gets you emotional? Happy, sad, angry?
5. What do you have that you are proud of? What do you regret?
6. How do you communicate?
7. How have you adapted your true self at work? Around your family?
8. How do you view yourself? How do you view self-love? How are you viewed by others?
9. Are you confident in your life's current direction? Why or why not?
10. What have you lied to yourself about?
11. What do you do out of fear, obligation, and guilt?
12. When are you happiest?
13. What primary motives drive your day-to-day life?
14. Are you jaded? In what areas?

This list could be a book by itself, so I will stop here. But this can get you started.

Set aside some real time to think: a thinking retreat, a retreat with just you and a notepad. Shut off the phone, and eliminate all distractions. Then it will be time to start answering some very important and often tough questions. Start with each area of your life: family, finance, career, faith/beliefs, friends, physical, and mental.

What do you believe about those things as they relate to your life? Why? Then ask why again and again. Usually it takes at least three whys to get to the root of any shaping belief.

Why do you get so angry when that happens? Why do you feel frustrated in that area? Why do you think that about money? Why do you believe that about marriage? Why haven't you taken better care of your body? Do you really believe it's important? and so on.

Do the same with the timeline of your life. Write down every memory in two categories: positive or negative. Yes, every memory in a giant timeline from your earliest memory until now. What themes do you see? Why do these themes exist? Do they still serve you? Do you miss some themes? Why do you miss them, and where did they go? What do you realize about your life story so far? Were all the best times of your life when you lived near the water? Why do you live in the desert now? Are all your biggest missteps made while drinking? Were they made from a place of fear, obligation, or guilt? What happened at all the crossroads of your life? Why did you take the road you took? Was it easier? Harder? Were all the worst times of your life around family? You get the idea.

Now, what are you going to take with you into the future? And from your story, what needs to be unpacked from your travel bags and left on the ground right here? Like a big jacket you've been carrying around even though you moved to the tropics, there are a lot of things in all of our lives that served us at one point and are no longer needed. Do you really need to be the funny guy in class anymore? Do you still need to be buzzed to talk to the opposite sex or have a good time like your nervous college self? Do you still need the attention of the opposite sex?

Do you still need to beat yourself up? Justify that family member's terrible actions? Say yes to everything? Say no to things you're afraid of or because someone else thinks you should? Why that college career? Did you really ever want to be a lawyer? Did you end up in this career by accident? Why did you think rich people are bad (did you read too much Charles Dickens)? Keep going and going until you've exhausted your beliefs and your life's story. Then it will be time to make some decisions about what needs to stay and what needs to go.

Bringing a coach into your life at this point is a great idea. Friends and family don't really work here. You may be surprised to know that often most of the reasons people don't go after the life they really want is because they listened too much to those who care the most about them. After all, the people we love want to see us safe, familiar, and in a controlled environment. That's not what we are going after here.

Now that you have the ingredients to your new life, it's time to start picking a destination for your future by building a list of "dreams" — get at least 100. These are dreams, not goals. Want a condo on the moon? Want to marry that rock star or be one yourself? Put it on the list. Use this as an exercise to expand your mind and realize how big the world is and that life really is long enough to change everything if you want to.

From here, build a crystal clear and inspiring vision of the most incredible life you can imagine. With a date on it. When will you arrive? Visualize this destination, and build a plan to make it happen. You were meant for more than you could ever imagine. Unfortunately, most people stay in a familiar, safe, and controlled environment and trade their dreams, their souls, and their ethos for it. But why? You are the only you the world will ever see.

Don't die without you seeing who you could really be. Don't be the person who dies looking into the mirror without ever seeing the real, truest, most vibrant, alive, passionate, and successful person you could be. This would be the greatest crime to humanity and ourselves.

Instead, take the time to discover who you are. Be that person to the greatest extent possible. And then, let whatever happens … happen. It just might change everything.

ABOUT CRAIG BOYD

A passionate, energetic, and enthusiastic leader and a committed high achiever, Craig Boyd's core belief is centered around the Growth Mindset. In a nutshell, this is the belief that skills and intelligence can be improved with effort and persistence. People with a Growth Mindset embrace challenges, stay resilient in the face of difficulties, learn from constructive criticism, and seek out inspiration from others' success. As a leader in business, this translates to the meta qualities of self-awareness and learning agility. These concepts have been the foundation of Craig's personal growth and success.

Growing up in a small country town in Australia, sports and education dominated his early years. The principles of the Growth Mindset, combined with dedication, hard work, and commitment, took him from a small business owner at the age of 23 to working in Kuala Lumpur and Bangkok, running some of Asia's best fitness centers. His work in the health and fitness industry enabled him to transition into a global role leading a successful U.S. pharmaceutical organization.

Drive and ambition challenged Craig to chase opportunities and new roles. His experience is diverse, having worked in various industries, countries, and companies. He has been happily married for nearly 30 years and has two amazing children.

5

EMBRACE THE GROWTH MINDSET

by
Craig Boyd

I grew up in a small, rural town just south of Sydney, Australia. It was a tough environment for me. My father left home when I was five. My mother raised my brother and me while working as a cleaner at a local school. Most of my classmates' parents were unemployed, as we relied on the fragile and declining coal-mining and steel-manufacturing industries to support our community. In fact, we did not have real cow's milk at home until I was 18. Today, when I look back, many of the people I went to school with are either dead, unemployed, or in prison.

In my youth, I believed I could make it as a professional rugby player and that would be enough. My love of sport was the best way for me to grow up and be least influenced by my surroundings. I was able to connect the dots of good coaching and hard work, which translated to results. However, I did not take my school work seriously and would often play as many sports as possible so that I could avoid the classroom. In hindsight, this was my mistake. Fortunately, testing came easy to me — akin to performing in a sporting event.

Through some encouragement of good coaches, I eventually found myself wanting to go to university to study to become a physical and health education teacher. The rationale for choosing to become a teacher was to ensure job security. That is, you would graduate and be employed by the government — essentially a job for life. This was to make certain that I avoided the unemployment pathway that I had experienced in my youth with most of my class-mates' fathers not having a job. I also became aware that a rugby career could end quickly if I became badly injured, so I needed to have a plan B.

Given my lack of attentiveness at school in the past, I had a monumental effort ahead of me to study hard in my final year to ensure I achieved the necessary grades to get into university — essentially cramming six years of work into my final year. The way I approached this challenge was intense — studying late at nights and on weekends when I was not playing rugby. As a strategy, I would spend the majority of my time studying past exam papers so that I became familiar with the types of questions that would be asked. On reflection, this was a good move and helped me achieve the grades needed to get into university.

I lived at home while attending university. Luckily, I had a class-mate who lived near me and I could ride with him to school. I also managed to start getting paid to play rugby and secured a part-time job at a local club. Now I was balancing rugby, a part-time job, and university — which was all fairly demanding.

During this time at university, I met all kinds of people who were ambitious, smart, and hardworking (very different from in my childhood). I also managed to meet my wife there (although it took me three years to convince her to have a date with me). She was an inspirational source of ongoing encouragement and support.

When I graduated from university, I was ranked as a top-ten student. However, much to my surprise, I was unable to get a job — that was not the plan. What had gone wrong ? How could this be the case? (For the record, my wife found employment.) This situation made me do something different.

I believed that I had to be in control of my future. I took initiative to make a change and somehow convinced my mother to help me with some money to put a deposit on a local fitness center. My mother did not have much, so I was conscientious of making this decision work and ensure she would not lose her money — no matter what. My wife-to-be was also a fantastic support person who helped me with this challenge, including using some of her salary to help pay the bills.

10 Ways to Embrace the Growth Mindset

My core belief is centered around being positive in the face of adversity. Through research, I later found out the official term for this is "Growth Mindset." In a nutshell, it is the belief that skills, intelligence, and results can be improved with effort and persistence. When I grew up, this was obvious to me in the sports I played. The hard work, training, and dedication give you the platform to win — however, you also need the belief that you are ready to win.

The other factors that go into this formula of success are the right coaches, mentors, and people you spend time with. People with a Growth Mindset embrace challenges, stay resilient in the face of difficulties, learn from constructive criticism, and seek out inspiration in others' success. Having a Growth Mindset is every-thing — your success begins and ends with mindset.

The lesson for life is embrace your Growth Mindset and the influences related to you (coaches, mentors, and friends). I have the Growth Mindset acronym that I'll share with you at the end of this chapter. Before that, however, I want to share ten ways I encourage you to embrace this concept for your self-improvement, growth, and success:

1. Have self-belief: Believe you can improve. Skills are not born — they are made.
2. Be a lifelong learner: Learning is important — embrace learning and reflect on what you have learned.
3. Embrace new opportunities that will take you out of your comfort zone.
4. If you don't know the answer, ask questions or find someone who knows.
5. Mistakes are okay and are part of learning.
6. Feedback and criticism should not be seen as "threats" — seek them out — and be thankful for such input. Use this to support you in your learning instead.
7. Be resilient — stick at it.
8. Your mindset has the ability to change throughout your life.
9. Seek out positive people such as coaches, mentors, leaders, and friends.
10. It's never too late to start!

Continuing to Learn and Grow

The opportunity to work for myself and accept the challenges of owning my own business straight out of university was a game changer. I had people who were willing to take a chance on me combined with my mindset of self-belief that I would make this a success — no matter what.

From my small fitness center out of university, within two years, I eventually found myself moving to Malaysia and later Thailand to operate ten fitness centers in both countries. Each step of this journey required me to get back to mindset. I needed to learn two different cultures (Muslim in Malaysia and Buddhist in Thailand), plus two different languages (Bahasa in Malaysia and Thai in Thailand).

At the conclusion of this three-year opportunity, my wife and I ran Asia's first International Fitness Convention and Trade Show (Bangkok, Thailand) in 1995 and then again in 1996. Our goal was to showcase the world's best fitness instructors and teachers to the Asian population so that they could learn and grow. This was a huge success — as was the same event the following year. And then, the conference was sold to a company in Hong Kong.

Our next plan was to return to Australia and start a family. This was also a success! Our daughter was born in 1997. And our son was born in 1999. However, when I got back down under, I needed to find a job. And so, I somehow found myself in the pharmaceutical industry — as encouraged by Dr. Mackay, who was our rugby club doctor for many years.

In Sydney, I went from primary care pharmaceutical sales rep to now being the president of a fast-growing U.S. pharmaceutical company based in Chicago. This 20-year journey advanced from my prior experiences, the MBA I earned, and my ongoing belief in myself that I could continue to learn and grow. My life continues to illustrate the Growth Mindset. And I hope it inspires you to do the same with yours!

M.I.N.D.S.E.T.: Some Good News

What's the good news? It's not too late to develop a Growth Mindset — it just takes a little practice.

However, simply telling someone to have a Growth Mindset can backfire. People can have a negative reaction to being told how to think. Instead, a more practical explanation about the brain — that it can get stronger and smarter with new learning — can be more effective to get "buy-in."

In the same vein, reiterating the message "Just try harder" can also be problematic, which is what most people hear. But a Growth Mindset isn't just about trying harder. We need to understand why we should put in more effort and how to deploy that effort. From what we know so far, sometimes a better strategy is more useful than additional effort spent doing the same thing. Invest time up front to understand the opportunity and risks, then formulate your winning strategy based on your key strengths.

Using the word "mindset" as an acronym, I have created a summary of key words:

- M — Learn from Mistakes
- I — Improve
- N — Never Give Up
- D — Determination
- S — Self-Awareness
- E — Effort
- T — Training

I have this acronym posted in my office. I also have it saved in a paper journal that I update regularly when I learn new things. These days, at work, I enjoy my leadership role of guiding and encouraging the team to strive. We are a fast growing U.S. pharmaceutical organization that has delivered an annual growth of more than 20 percent for the past five years, and we are considered a "Best Place to Work" by the global authority on workplace culture, Great Place to Work® (www.alwaysaheadseries.com). Establishing a foundation of Growth Mindset has positively impacted our culture and enabled both of these achievements.

I take active mentor roles with several people from around the world as I share my story. I listen to their story, and we decide together how the concepts of the Growth Mindset can best help them continue to enhance their career and themselves as a person. I feel this is the best part of the Growth Mindset — getting others to understand how it works and implement the tool set. Your brain has the ability to change throughout your life. Never stop learning.

ABOUT STUART M. CRAWFORD

 Stuart Crawford is a seasoned mortgage professional who has been in the mortgage banking business for ten years. His career started with Waterfield Financial, a leading private mortgage banking firm, where he was a top producing banker at the firm, working with the #1 top producing branch for the company nationwide.

Waterfield Financial was acquired by American Home Mortgage, a multi-billion dollar firm publicly traded on the NYSE. Prior to the unfortunate bankruptcy of the company, Stuart was ranked in the President's Club as a Top 100 producer out of 3,000 bankers nationwide.

Stuart then contributed to the success of V.I.P. Mortgage, after the company was founded in August of 2007. V.I.P. continues to be a leading mortgage company that saw astounding growth over the years during which its competitors struggled to survive — and it will continue to be a market leader as they're determined to "Restore the Reputation of the Mortgage Industry."

Today, at Bison Ventures, Stuart is committed to providing five-star, unmatched service in the mortgage industry to all of his clients. It's his priority to thoroughly educate his clients on all of their financing options so that the right product fit is achieved.

6

FIND YOUR VILLAGE

by
Stuart M. Crawford

It is human nature to want to continually evolve and grow, learning new things and challenging yourself to enter new chapters of life. This occurs for us personally and professionally as we seek purpose and fulfillment through this journey. Throughout my career, I can vividly remember the times when that burning gut feeling to "do something different" happened. To be clear, doing something different was not necessarily a career/industry change but simply growing into the next professional version of myself and having the feeling of "moving forward."

Born in San Antonio, I lived in Texas for nine years before moving to Albuquerque, New Mexico. After high school, I moved to Arizona to attend ASU, and I've been in the greater Phoenix area since. I started my mortgage career by default as a part-time job during my senior year at ASU. I was working in a small call center, cold-calling off lead sheets and trying to set appointments for loan officers. After graduation, I wanted to become a stock broker. While looking for my "real job" with my Finance degree, I continued to work in the mortgage space, eventually becoming a loan officer before the 2007 housing crisis. I quickly caught a bad taste as the people I worked for, along with the industry at that time, did not seem very professional — so I quit.

The struggle with this is the notion of leaving your comfort zone, as this is what is required to satisfy the feeling to move forward. Later in my career, when I was at my most successful — in terms of production and financial reward — I remember the overwhelming feeling of being burned out and not knowing if I could continue to push on day after day. The feeling was not just exhaustion but a deeper desire to change the script and sculpt the trajectory differently. This required letting go of full control and allowing others to directly help me with my business.

This is very common, and many of us get to a point where we simply need to delegate or hire to move certain responsibilities from our plate in order to maintain or scale with any version of sanity and life balance. The most recent example is when we launched our new company. Talk about leaving your comfort zone! This is a time when it feels you are leaving everything behind that you have done up until this point, and you are embarking on a daring and risky journey with no guaranteed outcome. Yet for some reason, even understanding the risks, something in your gut tells you it is the right thing to do and the right time to do it.

This unnatural notion of knowing you are leaving your comfort zone elicits a series of responses that have to be navigated and managed in order to stay the course. Specifically, the first internal reaction is self-doubt, and fear begins to rear its head. The fear that you made the wrong decision. The fear of failing for both yourself and those around you. The fear of imposter syndrome. I personally felt all these fears, and they began to control most of my thoughts. This effect caused me to doubt the very thing that I understood I was supposed to trust . . . my gut. All of a sudden, I began to challenge my intuition. And I became paralyzed about knowing how best to move forward.

When I was 22, a friend of mine convinced me to go back into the industry with a special company, promising it was different and would feel like the beginning of a real career. I quickly found this to be true and was fortunate to work alongside true, authentic professionals who would end up mentoring me and providing the foundation for my career. I had to overcome many challenges in the beginning since I was on 100 percent commission and had to battle my way into creating relationships and providing value to build up a network. There were many times I wanted to quit, but I somehow found the courage to push through via great leadership and support around me.

This was the moment I realized there is no reason to go about this alone and that with the right people around me, I could possibly gain the clarity needed to move forward. When you find this village, everything can change, but how do you find it?

Be Open & Vulnerable

You must have trust in your journey and believe in yourself and the path you are on. This will provide the comfort needed in uncomfortable times. What I have learned is that in many cases, in order to accomplish this, you cannot feel like you are on an island. Meaning, you have nobody to relate to — or you feel that whatever is occurring in your business or life is only happening to you. This is powerful, and it amazes me how quickly an individual's senses can change once they realize they are not alone — and that they most definitely do not have to go it alone.

For me, I needed to find a way to trust and believe that letting go and giving myself permission to grow and change was the right thing to do. I can relate this lesson to a few times over my career, but the most significant was the idea of starting a new company. Although my intuition told me it was in fact the right course for the next chapter, once it became real, I had to determine (a) how to find comfort where it did not exist, and (b) how to battle the "naysaying" on a daily basis.

In these moments, I found myself devoting most of my energy to pretending that these feelings were not happening and showing the outside world that everything was fine. Of course, this is normal as we build the wall to insulate ourselves from what we perceive is the fear of judgment or protecting ourselves from something we may not want to hear. I realized I no longer trusted my own judgment. This is when I decided to once again "let go" and bring others into the conversation so that I could gain more knowledge and insight to help chart the course.

You must be open and vulnerable in order to grow. This is also required to be authentic and to have real conversations with those you trust. So many of us lock up with fear or the idea that we are seen as weak in these moments, when the reality is, we are strongest in these moments — if we take the correct action to put an army around us. Typically, these are "high stakes" changes in our lives, and the idea that we would go it alone is simply crazy. It takes courage to let our pride down and to engage in brutally honest conversations with those around us.

Once you begin to open up, you will quickly find that your experiences are shared and there is a massive dose of comfort in not only knowing others have been through this but that they grew from it as well. The whole point is that we want to grow, and we have to understand that sometimes to achieve the growth we seek, we have to move through uncomfortable zones. Although, these zones do not have to be lonely, nor should they be. I love to share experiences, and I love to laugh. The more people in your village, the more of these good feelings are going to happen.

Finding this is simple; we just have to start with those closest to us and work our way out from there. It can start with a close friend, family member, spouse, member, or colleague. I would challenge you to have three truly open conversations with individuals from your inner circle and see if you can find another three from there. Your village can be as small or large as you feel comfortable with — there are no rules. There are plenty of people who love to share and guide, and it becomes fun to bring others on your journey.

Finding My Village

After the first year, at 23, I began to have small successes with fostering some key relationships that helped propel my production and gave me the transactional experience I desperately needed. I achieved a top producer status based on the company's standards. Then, in the midst of an 18-month span, our company was sold to a much larger company that was publicly traded on the NASDAQ …

After this, we went from 300 loan officers to 3,000. And then this company was one of the first big mortgage banks to go under in the summer of 2007 — at the tip of the toxic housing crisis. This was a scary time, and I did not know where things would go from there.

In that paralyzing moment when I doubted my own intuition, I had to be proactive and find a way to break free and regain the belief and confidence required to evolve into the next version of myself. In order to accomplish this, I had to find others who were willing to invest their time and support with me. As I began to open up and have these conversations, I found that it quickly led to a handful of close relationships with people who were swift to want to engage and show their love and support. I feel very fortunate that I cannot single one individual out, as there are many.

Their investment was genuine care and a desire to provide what was needed in those challenging moments. This starts with a sincere listener, then morphs into a sounding board for the real input needed to help navigate what lies in front of you. Time is our most valuable asset, so you can imagine how grateful you would feel when others invest their own time into supporting you.

Furthermore, you want to be sure you use this to take the actions required to be successful in the journey. If these special individuals were going to invest in me, I surely did not want to let them down. I took all the information and did my best to pour it into my routine, with the goal of having confidence in my purpose and the intuition that got me to that point to begin with.

After successfully navigating from the paralysis moment, it became clear that going through this not only helped me grow, but it created a foundation for me to have the ability to help others along their way. I found myself thinking a lot about my children and how impactful it could be in the future if they were going through their own "chapter changes" and how this experience alone gave me enough firsthand insight to help guide them. Today, I find so much comfort in knowing I can say, "Son, I get it, and let me tell you a story …"

This village around me had a profound impact on my life. Not for the obvious reason of helping with a specific challenge but for the greater picture of having an understanding of how powerful community is, and how much it can positively shape your surroundings. The people of your village help you achieve the ultimate feeling in uncomfortable times, which gives you the confidence and strength you need to believe in yourself and trust in your journey. This lesson is so important, as it can relate to any aspect of your life, and it can be applied to any situation that calls for the desire to feel grounded again.

Grounded & Pushing Through

At some point, many of us will find ourselves in need of a change. The bigger the desire for change, the more that "pilot flame" burns bright. We must act on this and not let the flame get out of control. This change is a part of our life's journey in which we choose to leave one chapter and enter a new one. Just the thought of leaving a comfort zone and going into the unknown is enough to hinder most people from ever making the real moves necessary to truly experience life. It is so important we push through, and we find the courage to bring as many into the story as we can.

After my previous employers closed shop, my mentor at the time decided to start a mortgage company with his childhood friend, and they asked me to join them. We started with about ten people, and the company grew to over 500 employees over the next 14 years. At this company, I was a consistent President's Club award winner, eventually ranking in the top three spots in the company for personal production, year after year. I also became an owner in the company and took on more senior leadership/executive responsibilities.

By finding others to invest in you, you are absolutely investing in yourself. The more we practice the art of progressing forward, the better we get at it. As you leave one comfort zone and realize it all worked out, you gain the confidence to do it again and again. Not only does this allow you to grow as an individual and fight complacency, but it also offers you a gift that you can give to those around you who find themselves in a place where it is needed most.

After 15 years of working with my mentor, I finally decided it was time to start my own legacy and create a new company/brand that had a deeper meaning for me personally. Bison Ventures launched in March of 2023, and I am currently enjoying the journey of learning every day and building something that provides opportunity for our employees and our families.

In my personal experience, continually leaving your comfort zone is only possible by building your village and surrounding yourself with the right people to cheer you on along the way. Plus, who wants to travel the journey without any laughter? Well, you need someone to laugh with — so go find them!

3RD QUARTER

As you enter the third quarter of your career, this is one of the most valuable times for you to start setting yourself up for the rest of your life. You'll have so many experiences, through education and investing back into yourself. In Quarters #1 and #2, you were spending so much time honing your skills in order to now begin accruing wealth that you can pass on from generation to generation. You've been shown how you're a number one asset, and by now you hopefully feel like that's true.

If you're a professional athlete, you're pretty much retired from your sport. You have all this financial wealth you have accrued, to the point that you have to figure out how to invest. This is a time for finding property, business, and foundations to support.

If you're not a professional athlete, it's likely that you've already tried three or four jobs. Now you're into your final career that you love — your true calling. At this stage, investing your time is absolutely key. The one thing we all have equal in a day is time — 24 hours. Hopefully, from the first 20 years of working, you've learned the importance of time management, you've found at least one good mentor, and you have invested back into yourself. With those factors in place, you're now prepared to set up the rest of your life.

As you go through your career, you will have stepped into being a number one asset. To reflect, you should have become adept in the following:

1. Time management (it's vital to continual growth)
2. Business acumen (this should have grown exponentially)
3. Expertise (as well as loving what you do)

As you further invest in your career to set yourself up for the fourth quarter, in my opinion, you should be attending national conferences at least twice a year to further hone your skills. Also, as you network with other professionals in your field, you should be considering who you might want to work with in a consulting capacity. I fully recommend considering a true coach who will take you to the next level.

If you look at any true professional, they often have business coaches throughout their experience. When you're an athlete, you usually start off with coaches. In the very beginning, it's usually a parent. Then you get into clubs, sports, and high school, where you have a coach. In college, you have another coach. And then when you make it to the majors or professional level, you have different coaches. You have athletic trainers. You have the main head coach. You have assistant coaches. You also have coaches who work on your athleticism, agility, and so on.

When you're in the third quarter of your life, you're setting up for the final quarter of your career. So, finding the right coach is important. By now, you've probably already had one to three coaches — your mentors. They helped you during a time in which you were acquiring education and trying different jobs in order to find your true calling. Now that you're aligned with your career, you need a coach who will help you find your true potential — so you can properly invest in yourself.

As the third quarter is between the ages of 41 and 55, this really is during your peak wealth and growth years. You have more than a decade to accumulate all that wealth. For a professional athlete, this stage would really take place between 21 and 35 — closer to the second quarter for the rest of us. For career-oriented individuals — doctors, attorneys, accountants, real estate agents, lenders, brokers, plumbers, contractors, and so on — this stage is your sweet spot for investing back in yourself.

People have shown you that you're a number one asset while you made your way to this quarter. You're now learning how you can show the world that this is true. This is the time to charge a higher rate because of all your years of experience. By the time you enter your fourth quarter, you should be crawling in wealth. Not only that, while investing in yourself, you should also begin investing in your generational wealth as well.

ABOUT JEREMY SCHUBERT

 Jeremy is an accomplished and versatile Global Business Leader with a 30-year track record of innovation and performance excellence. Jeremy's experience with international health systems coupled with his MPH have enabled him to master both Health Economic and Public Health Strategy … this is further activated by his unique ability to craft and communicate aspirational vision, while simultaneously outlining a clear, innovative road map for internal and external execution.

Jeremy is known as a Business Builder with a proven ability to facilitate the development of a healthy, high-performance culture and construct new approaches and thinking to age-old problems.

Jeremy holds a degree in Marketing from Texas A&M University, an MBA from Northwestern's Kellogg School of Management, and an MPH from Liverpool University in England. He is completing a Doctorate of Strategic Leadership at Liberty University.

7

BBQ SAUCE CURIOSITY

by
Jeremy Schubert

I was watching television with my son one night. *Ted Lasso*, to be exact. The episode we were watching triggered my recall of a fond and important life lesson for success. The scene is one where the protagonist (Ted) is pulled into a dart-throwing contest with Rupert, the former owner of Ted's soccer club. The bet proposed is that if Ted loses, Rupert gets to choose his starting lineup, with potential dire consequences to the club. The start of the scene is chock-full of Rupert's bravado and arrogance regarding Ted's abilities and essentially challenging those as well as Ted's relevance as a football coach. Rupert is world class at darts.

At the end of the match, Ted is left with the need to hit two triple twenties and a bullseye to win. It doesn't look good for ol' Ted for sure. As Ted steps up to take his last three throws to a sarcastic "good luck" from Rupert, he begins a soliloquy that offers a deep insight for success. He starts by highlighting how he'd been underestimated and ridiculed all of his life and then … hits everyone with a life truth often attributed to Walt Whitman:

"Be curious, not judgmental."

He continues to explain his life epiphany that not one person who underestimated him was ever curious about him. They never asked him any questions, like "Have you played a lot of darts, Ted?" He speaks while hitting two triple twenties, continuing with, "Which I would have answered, 'Yes sir, every Sunday afternoon at a sports bar with my father from age 10 'til I was 16 when he passed away.'" He takes a deep breath and says his winning mantra, "BBQ Sauce," while throwing the final bullseye.

"Be curious, not judgmental" is profound because at face value, it is common sense, just not common practice. The insight here is that Ted's words not only allude to being curious about the outside world or other people but also are a subtle nuanced directive to be curious about ourselves … knowing ourselves. After all, there is no shortage of "haters" for people seeking great success. However, I think the more interesting point is that generally speaking, the biggest underestimator of our abilities is usually ourselves.

I had to learn this lesson without the guidance of Ted Lasso, but from a better and more real person: Phil Styrlund, CEO, mentor, and friend. I have been blessed to be a successful MedTech executive for the span of my 30-year career. I hit a crossroads about 20 years in, where I found that how I saw the world was much different from my peers and those senior to me. Of course, this created a ton of friction as I shared a view of the business and the direction in which I thought it should go that was not only uncommon … it was ununderstood.

My different view and personality resulted in pushback bordering on ridicule as those whom I worked both with and for stared blankly — and with judgment — at the picture I was painting. My frustration was high, and doubt began to creep in. Despite the fact that our team was consistently delivering better than any other, I was unhappy and frustrated, and it was impacting my health and relationships. Then late one Thursday afternoon, Phil brought to me some advice steeped in wisdom: "Jeremy, you have some unique and powerful gifts … that of insight and foresight. I encourage you to tap into your curiosity about those gifts … why you have them and how you are intended to use them."

Three Questions of Self Curiosity

The key lesson Phil was imparting is that personal power requires personal curiosity to unlock it. Personal power and purpose are very deep subjects. There are entire disciplines that attempt to explore and explain both. Although I don't pretend to know all the secrets of each, I can summarize the path to unlocking them through three basic questions.

1. What do you find meaningful?
2. What gifts do you have?
3. How are you "using" goals to align gifts with meaning?

What do you find meaningful?

Humans are "meaning" machines. At our lowest level, we consume meaning. It's how we make sense of the world … attempting to understand and internalize what people say and do, and how they act. At a higher level, we create meaning. It's how we influence the world — through our actions, contributions, and treatment of others … including how we treat ourselves.

In order to be successful, you have to identify what you find meaningful. After all, isn't that the essence of success? Achieving personal meaning? Without clarity here, making money, winning games, living large, and so on may all be exceptional outcomes that equate to very little self-actualization in the end. You have to know you experience meaning to experience true success. I was told once that you have two birthdays. The first is the day you were born and the second is the day you realize why you were born. So many people never live to see Day 2. Success mandates you sit down and define what you personally find meaningful.

What gifts do you have?

I don't care who you are or what spiritual underpinning you may choose; the fact is there is only one you. You are uniquely designed with capabilities and skills (visible and latent) that will enable you to live aligned to the meaning outlined above. In fact, the things you find meaningful are inextricably connected to the talents you possess … those you know and those that you have not yet discovered.

The goal of this question is to encourage you to be curious about your gifts. I intentionally use the word "gifts" here, as I believe there is power in seeing our abilities through that lens. It helps us understand that our gifts shouldn't be taken for granted and frames them in a vale of gratitude. We all are familiar with the concept of being "in the zone" … this is no more complicated than when we are fully living in and leveraging our strengths as gifts.

The importance here is that it's difficult to fully enjoy life if you are not optimizing the use of your talents. I personally believe we are hardwired with a desire to unearth and use our personal gifts. The Bible directs as much in the Parable of the Talents. Although one of the best ways to get at this is through the feedback of others (i.e., what others say you are good at), it's important to invest time in self-reflection.

Oftentimes, a gift is buried deep inside your psyche and just hasn't experienced the catalyst that would unlock it. Take time to know and name your gifts. You can't experience success without using your gifts … you can experience more success if you know what those gifts are.

How are you "using" goals to align gifts with meaning?

I'm guessing no book or article on success can go without some mention of goals or objectives. There is more research than necessary to articulate here on why goals are important, but I want to offer a different reason for asking yourself the question. It's based on something I read years ago: "Successful people don't **have** goals, they **use** goals."

Now, over the years, I've found this simple statement very powerful for me but often a throwaway for others. Here is the point … achievement of the goal is a weak and unfulfilling definition of success. Achieving a goal in such a way that simultaneously leverages your gifts and creates the experience of meaning is genuine success.

Unfortunately, goals are often viewed as endpoints — things we meet or achieve that become virtual awards in the mental trophy cabinet. However, goals can be used to align our time to what we find meaningful and as a planning tool for identifying how to use our gifts in the optimal way. Said another way, there are many paths to achieving a goal. Finding the path that leverages gifts and creates meaning requires the question of how we can "use" the goal. Even when goals are handed to us by our boss or company (as happens all too often in business), the call to action still should be to be very clear with ourselves how we will use said goals just as outlined above.

Curiosity Is a State of Being

Now, at a time when many want to fancy themselves as Servant Leaders, it may seem that operating with a curiosity of self is narcissistic — especially when you consider the desperate need this world has for Servant Leadership. I would argue this "curiosity of self" is actually a prerequisite to genuinely becoming a Servant Leader.

For those of us who travel quite a bit, we can probably all recite the safety instructions airlines go through prior to takeoff.

The directive is first to "put on your oxygen mask before helping others." This is not "me first" mentality. It is directed to ensure you are in a state of being to help others. By working through this "self-curiosity" process, you are putting on the proverbial mask of Servant Leadership enablement. My mentor and friend Phil Styrlund often uses another statement that just might be a better analogy: "You can't give away what you don't have."

For you to meaningfully help others, you have to enable yourself to come from a point of strength and peace. Another way to look at it is that curiosity is a state of being … it's not an event or moment. By consistently reviewing these questions for ourselves, we become naturally curious about others. Once we start to view and know others through their view of meaning and gifts, we can be much more useful in helping them use goals to get the most out of life.

We all have an obligation to bring our best selves to work, relationships, and life in general. You can't be your best self and positively impact the world if you live incongruently to meaning and your gifts. It's just that simple.

Coaching Others & BBQ Sauce

Back to Phil. He was the first to encourage me to look within. I really thought I knew myself … and for the most part I did. What I did not realize was how incongruent my life and perspective were becoming with how I experienced meaning and how I was using or viewing my gifts. I couldn't see how I was poisoning myself with the feedback of others.

Phil invested hours mentoring me through unlocking my internal meaning and gifts, better management, and interpreting the environment around me. He didn't stop at the surface. He lovingly and methodically guided me to unpack meaning and gifts and to use goals to find my feet again. Like most coaches, Phil understood the need for him to be curious about me. However, Phil did what only elite coaches do: he taught me how to be curious about myself so that I could be the best version of me for this world and the people I care about.

As Phil and other elite coaches read the summary of meaning, unique gifts, and using goals ... I can't help but think that, much like Ted Lasso, they are all whispering "BBQ Sauce."

Much Love and Good Luck

So, in summary ... take the time to really write out where you find meaning. Dig deep to evaluate your strengths and label them as gifts. Set and use personal goals to ensure you align your gifts with where you find meaning, and translate any goals you are given to do the same. Doing these three simple things will elevate you toward genuine success in life.

If you are looking for other BBQ Sauce insights, I would highly recommend you check out Phil's book, *Relevance: Matter More*. It covers this and much, much more. Godspeed, and much love to you all!

ABOUT JASON BOYER

Jason Boyer is an architect, developer, and the founder of Boyer Vertical.

Boyer's strength is resilience — possessing an entrepreneurial skill set that is both design and business savvy. At age 35, Boyer was named Design Principal in a national architectural firm, a notable accomplishment in a profession where the average principal age is 52. In 2012 Boyer established Jason Boyer Architects, adding real estate development to his skill set. His first development project was the award-winning artHAUS condominiums in Midtown Phoenix. He has since transformed his practice to focus on design-led real estate development, re-establishing it as Boyer Vertical in 2020. Boyer Vertical integrates architecture, development, and construction under a single real estate platform focused on creating sustainable-minded, architecturally significant projects.

Boyer serves as architectural studio instructor at the ASU Design School and guest lecturer to the ASU Master of Real Estate Development program. His work in the "Architect as Developer" realm has spurred a following of architects who seek his counsel. Jason Boyer received the national honor of being named one of the 2022 Class of Fellows by the American Institute of Architects (AIA), a recognition earned by only 4 percent of national AIA member architects, which number more than 94,000.

8

THREE STRIKES

by
Jason Boyer

In baseball, three strikes and you're out, yet the next at bat brings new opportunity. In soccer, one team can dominate possession but struggle to hit the back of the net only to find themselves beaten by a single opposing player's will to win. In the pool, a swimmer trains for months on end, building the strength, endurance, and flexibility to compete, and yet it's their ability to handle pressure and maintain focus in competition that determines the outcome. I frame what I'm about to tell you in this way because I've taken valuable lessons from sport that I use in life and business every day.

As an extroverted introvert, I can tell you straight-out that my path to sustainable entrepreneurial self-confidence did not come easily. It was built around the discipline I take from sport and failures I've experienced in business that became some of my biggest triumphs in life. I've struggled to separate the two for most of my adult life and often overindulge the business side. I'm good at work;

I'm great at getting shit done. I'm a driver. I'm not always so good when it comes to empathy and placing my friends and family over work.

My mindset was always "Work hard; do whatever it takes for the first 10 years of my career, and I'll be set up for success." I worked harder but not always smarter. In the early days of my career, I'd disappear from life outside of work for months at a time, wholly focused on the project at hand — grinding out 60- to 80-, or even 100-hour weeks, one after the other. Project after project, year after year, I hit the completion point. Deadline met. Result achieved. But there was a cost.

Reintegrating life outside work became awkward at times. Looking back, I can't help but think I was feeling some form of PTSD … I literally fell asleep at my own 30th birthday party — something my wife and friends love to revisit on occasion.

In the summer of 2020, I was enjoying a month-long working beach vacation, as my wife and I had come to define it. A few years back, I had read an article that touted the benefits of a prolonged family summer vacation, noting it takes one full week to unwind from the grind, the second and third weeks to relax and connect deeply with family, while the fourth and final week leaves you energized, with a desire to return to work.

I inserted this page into my annual routine several years ago. Not only that, I share the recommendation often with other people. Living in Arizona, a change of scenery in the depths of the summer heat has become a must in my game of life.

Occasionally something interrupts this flow. And Monday morning, July 13, 2020, became one of those moments. My day started on routine with an early morning workout followed by a cup of coffee as I looked out over the waves dotted by the morning surf crew. I jumped on a video call at 8 a.m. It was my weekly partner meeting, and one of my three partners asked if my family was in the room.

Odd, I thought to myself. A few minutes later, I understood what he was after.

That morning, I was fired …

Three Gifts of Change

For the third time in ten years, I found myself on the receiving end of a goodbye "gift." My first two "gifts" were received in the years preceding, and then July 13th was an important threshold for me. Three strikes and I was out. Each "gift" was a pain point I'll never forget. Each offered a hurdle to something better on the other side — something unknown but more aligned with my own sense of self-worth that would shape my journey to sustainable entrepreneurial self-confidence. Now, that's not to say the transformation was instantaneous. My path through the woods would be carved through recurring self-doubt and soul-searching work/life events that shaped who I would become.

"Gift" #1

In October 2006, I started a new position as the Phoenix office Design Director for a national architecture firm. Less than six months into the job, I was in the Chicago office boardroom on a blistering cold February morning opposite my firm's senior leadership team. The Phoenix office was struggling, and I knew where the brown spots were on the grass. I would leave this meeting wrapped in a cloak of newfound advocacy. Whatever I was doing was working in their eyes. They would empower me to be the changemaker.

Five projects, completed by five people, in a five-year period. That was the formula for winning new architectural commissions in the eyes of most clients. The core team of people I built could now check those boxes. We had crossed the threshold, and the results were good, if not great. We were building something special, and the core team saw the value that would come to each of them from our efforts. But something else was brewing. Something is always brewing ...

In September 2009, it was announced our firm was to be acquired. The merger and acquisition world was new to me, as it was to most partners back then. Not new were the brown spots that would soon appear on the green grass promised land sold to my advocates in Chicago.

A few months later, I was reporting to a new Jekyll and Hyde duo of micromanagers in Los Angeles. Nearly two years later, my plane landed at LAX, and I soon arrived at the Western Region Principal meeting site, a few blocks from the LA office, only to be redirected to the LA office boardroom. There, I found Jekyll and Hyde, along with the echo of HR on the phone, letting me know they were ready to cut my cord.

I was the golden boy, while executing a masterful turnaround play in under three years during a period marked by the Great Recession. The year following the merger, my team had interviewed for fourteen new building commissions, finished second place eight times, and won only one new major design commission.

The managers knew nothing of what I had achieved prior. They knew only the present batting average. The landscape had shifted, and my advocates were focused elsewhere. I protected my team but grossly underestimated the advocacy I would need to succeed in the new firm structure.

December 2011 saw the depth of the recession in Phoenix. Following the boardroom meeting, I found myself sitting in an LA hotel lobby with terminated iPhone service. My gut was in a knot. I was in disbelief and devastated. I had worked so hard and achieved so much. How could this happen to me? I felt lost ... again. After processing my anger and frustration at being unjustly dismissed, I felt something very different — a sense of freedom. I saw the gift this moment provided, forcing me to take a break from the frenetic pace of work and travel to spend nearly a year forming the strongest of bonds with my newborn daughter.

The tipping point was coming. I was certainly employable but didn't like the options available to me. An all-too-familiar corporate architecture leadership position surfaced early with an attractive compensation package. I interviewed for positions on the East and West Coasts, but nothing felt right.

My guard was up, and I wanted to preserve the newfound freedom and time I was gifted with my young family. Ultimately, it was my early focus on projects and people that led to an unexpected opportunity from a former client who offered a lifeline. This would become the foundation for my next steps.

"Gift" #2

Jason Boyer Architects was born in early 2012. I made my first hires pulling from the team I had built prior, purchased startup gear, and leased office space. Within months more opportunities surfaced with common threads linked to trusted relationship investments in my past.

Some people are Leaders, some are Doers, some are Connectors, others are Followers. My first real estate development project, artHAUS, was initiated by a "Connector" believing in my ability as an architect. artHAUS is a highly successful and award-winning 25-unit residential condominium urban infill project in Midtown Phoenix. Its path from concept to completion is a story unto itself, but its actualization stemmed from a singular question rooted in risk: Do I believe in myself?

Believing in yourself requires perseverance and determination to pursue your goals, despite unknown challenges and untold setbacks. Would you risk, would you actually guarantee, a $5 million construction loan for an upside of $1 million? Stop or believe. A simple choice bracketed by complex financial consequences and catapulting personal and professional growth opportunities. The outcome of this moment would shine a new light on what I could achieve, setting the vision for a design-led real estate development practice.

In early 2016, I entered "the Space Between." Here I was invited to join a nationally recognized firm as Principal. On the surface, it seemed a good fit. The firm sought my large project portfolio, established client relationships, and a track record in the Architect as Developer space. I considered the emerging practice to maintain a connection to my past project work and viewed the firm's support for my vision of design-led development as being in alignment with my professional goals.

The opportunity felt familiar and safe, something I initially welcomed. During my tenure, the firm was named AIA Arizona Firm of the Year and recognized by *Architect Magazine* in the ARCHITECT 50 for years 2017 and 2018. I directed the firm's large building commissions and successfully secured a highly competitive selection as 1 of 16 architecture firms from a field of 146 for the U.S. State Department Overseas Building Operations Embassy and Consulate program. It was a game-changing win for the firm and something I'm super proud of accomplishing.

Three Gifts (and I was out ...)

Despite my contributions, nearly six years of my focus and dedication to the growth and success of the partnership was undone in the first ten minutes of that Monday morning partner call. Our relationship had unraveled slowly due to a misalignment of expectations. We grew further apart with the onset of COVID-19 in 2020 as the distance provided a lens to widen our differing perspectives.

I had come into the firm during its downturn. They needed me ... I brought work and resources, provided the spark to land new strategic commissions, and shared my best assets that moved the firm to recession-proof status, poised for success. However, we were at odds as to how success would be maintained. And missing was the advancement of my professional goals. Partnerships are complicated. But in the dissolution of this partnership, I learned a life-changing lesson: never again would I put the goals of others in front of my own.

The summer of 2020 would deliver the final gift I needed to see the light. I had to set aside those familiar feelings of frustration and anger to realize this pain point was different. My own self-doubt had put me right back in the place I'd been before, and I had only myself to blame. I had failed to advocate for my own self-interest, failed to believe in my own ability.

By choosing financial security, comfort, and familiarity, I had failed to focus on my own goals. With clarity, I can now say I was scared, and it was this fear of failure that had held me back from my eventual path, despite the success of my first solo development project. My wife loves to remind me that "Everything happens for a reason." And the wisdom in her statement reveals that you should fully embrace the circumstances of life — never looking back, always looking ahead.

Carrying My Gifts Forward

I needed to go through each of these three life experiences to gain the sustained self-confidence to take control of my own circumstance … putting my goals first and activating my accumulated ability to advocate for my own self-interests. This required a mindset shift:

Be relentlessly focused on your goals.

Say NO … to anything not aligned with your goals.

Understand your success working toward others' goals can just as easily be working toward your own.

- Embrace your fears — let them fuel your success.
- Find your advocate.
- Advocate for others.
- Take actions that advocate for yourself.
- Create your own path, stick to it, and don't look back.
- Believe relentlessly … in yourself.

On occasion, I stumble across things worth sharing. The book *Little Black Stretchy Pants (The Unauthorized Story of Lululemon)* by Chip Wilson was a gift from my wife in 2019. It offers three big ideas:

1. See into the future
2. Be different on purpose
3. And fail, learn, repeat

The book showcases ordinary people who took the opportunity to be creative, to be innovative, and to maximize their potential. I found it inspirational!

I'm conscious of the encouragement and support I've received from others and overwhelmed by the following of architects who have come forward seeking my advice in the Architect as Developer arena. I'm not the first, and I don't have it all figured out. Every day brings new hurdles.

This way of business is HARD. It's incredibly testing and will teach you a lot about yourself. To succeed you must be willing to fail, you must find the grit for continuous improvement, and you must be resilient in the face of constant change.

Resilience is my superpower. What's yours?

Boyer Vertical, established in 2020, was conceived from a singular design-led real estate development concept eight years earlier. artHAUS delivered on the promise of great architecture, in a great location at an attainable price point. Today, with the completion of my second development project, KARMA, the firm's business eco-system forms a positive, self-perpetuating platform focused on creating sustainable architecturally significant projects in Arizona.

ABOUT LAUREN BAILEY

 Lauren Bailey is the CEO and co-founder of Upward Projects, a restaurant development and hospitality company known for one thing — making people feel good. Spanning over 25 restaurants and 5 brands across 5 states, Upward Projects is comprised of the Postino WineCafe, Joyride Taco House, Windsor, Churn Ice Cream, and Federal Pizza brands. Selected to the *Nation's Restaurant News* "Power 50" list of people who represent the best in restaurant leadership, Bailey and Upward Projects are regarded for developing first-rate culture and adapting and reusing historically relevant buildings that are an integral part of the neighborhoods they serve. The company has also been named to the Inc. 5000 list for multiple years as one of the nation's fastest-growing companies.

Texas-born and Indiana-raised, Lauren graduated from ASU with dual degrees in Communication and Fine Art. Drawing upon her degree, Lauren is also intimately involved in the design and décor of each Upward Projects location, from guiding the design direction to conceiving and executing the custom "art walls" that adorn each and every Postino WineCafe. In her spare time, Lauren travels the world, chases her eight-year-old son, hunts for vintage treasures, creates art, cooks dinner for friends, and spends time with the most important people in her life.

9

THE WINDSHIELD THEORY

by
Lauren Bailey

The ticking of my turn signal was the only thing breaking through the overwhelming silence of my car. Ironic, because my brain was working overtime — analyzing every move I'd made that day. *How did an 11-hour day go by in a blink? How had I gone from being a waitress to running this big company with more than 2,000 people depending on me? Did I respond to that email from my CFO? I think I screwed up that meeting.* A loud "HONNNNKKK" broke my mental rewind, and I looked back to see how angry the guy in the car behind me was as I joined the stream of cars racing home.

The next morning, I waited for Sam Fox in his office, feeling certain he was going to tell me exactly what I needed to do during this crazy growth period — including each and every thing he had done wrong while building his incredible empire — so that I could make sure I didn't make the same mistakes. He was chugging a Fiji water and comparing two very similar green paint swatches, while passionately discussing something with his Chief Legal Officer — the incomparable "Velvet Hammer," Leezie Kim.

Sam plopped down and began firing questions at me. "How are sales? What's happening with construction?" He asked what I thought about this or that. I was half shocked that he wanted to know any of this from me and half wanting to get at what I needed to know. Where did he go wrong along the way?

"So what's up; what do you need?" he finally said.

"Well, I'd really love to know what you feel your biggest mistakes were while you were growing — especially in the early high-growth years."

He looked at me as if I had asked him to repeat the theory of relativity. "What? What do you mean?"

I shifted around in my chair. "You know … where did you go wrong? What do you wish you would have done differently? I really need to know this."

I'd barely got the words out, when he said with total conviction, "Lauren, I don't sit around thinking about what mistakes I made or what I would have done differently yesterday. I'm focused on what I can improve *today*. I'm figuring out how I can make that menu better, what my team needs, and how I can get the deals I want. I get a finite number of hours today, and I'm not spending them on the past."

I was without a rebuttal. Which is rare. How can something so simple be so difficult? We wrapped up, and he left me with a powerful slap on the back that somehow conveyed "You've got this!" and "Don't screw it up," all at the same time.

I slogged back to my car, trying to figure out how I was going to work like this. I turned the key and checked my rearview mirror. At that moment, I realized that there is a reason the windshield is substantially larger than the rearview mirror. I am not getting anywhere safely if I am trying to drive forward looking behind me. The Windshield Theory was born.

The Windshield Theory

Since that day, I decided I would be maniacally focused on what I could do moving forward. I'll look back when I need to and understand the past, but only so that it can inform the future. Nearly every situation benefits from this approach. This practice has proved harder some days than others.

The past is comfortable. Overly dissecting situations and ruminating on prior events and assigning blame is often easier than trying to solve problems or optimize situations. Being future-focused almost always helps things move forward faster, better, and with more impact.

The Windshield Theory approach applies to our leadership approach with people and also how we each manage our internal narrative. First, I will focus on a leadership example and how keeping teams focused on forward thinking is fruitful — especially when they get off track.

An interpersonal example:

Jill works in the graphic design department of her company. She reports to Kira, who is the Chief Marketing Officer. Jill has been a great employee for many years, but as of late, she has begun gossiping and causing problems with other members of the team as a way of addressing her dissatisfaction and frustration with not getting a promotion. As a result, her work is slipping, and her execution and quality are deteriorating. As Kira witnessed Jill's decline, she was extremely frustrated, and several members of the team have come to her frustrated. It is affecting the overall health of the team and the company's results.

Scenario A:

Kira asks Jill to join her in her office.

"Look, Jill, I've been hearing from a bunch of people that you have been complaining about the company and gossiping about people," Kira begins. "And you haven't met many of the project deadlines the last few weeks," she continues. "This just can't continue."

Jill is visibly upset and begins to mentally review who she has been speaking to and what she has been saying, and she begins to prepare her defense.

"Who said that?" Jill stammers. "I missed that deadline because I didn't receive Caleb's brand standards on time!"

Kira gets lost in her own fact reporting, and they begin to talk in circles about what has transpired and why, and what has or has not occurred. She finds herself getting distracted defending others and trying to justify her own decision making. The conversation continues to ramp up, and Jill begins to accuse Kira of "having it in for her." Jill storms out of Kira's office.

Scenario B:

Kira reaches out to Jill to schedule a touch base and lets her know she wants to talk about her development.

"Jill, I've noticed that things don't appear to be the same with you, and I'd like to understand what's going on and share expectations on both sides," she says. "You've been a huge part of this team for a long time, and I really rely on you. Can I first ask if there is anything going on that you would like to discuss?"

Jill says softly, "Well, honestly, I am bummed about not getting the promotion — I really felt like I was ready and deserved it."

"Ah, I understand, and I can see why that is upsetting to you. I definitely should have reached out to you when it happened, and I'm sorry about that. Would it be all right with you if I shared what I need from you moving forward to be eligible for a promotion?"

Jill replies, "Sure."

"It's really important that everyone on the team is positive and supports one another and, if there is an issue, that we bring it up and discuss it and plan for how we can move on. Can I trust that from now on, if there is something that is bothering you or you don't agree with, you'll discuss it with me first? I will commit to doing the same with you," says Kira.

"Yes, I suppose I can do that."

"Great," says Kira. "I also want to know that you are in a position to focus all of your energy on executing your projects and meeting the timelines we agree to as a group. Can I ask you for that?"

"Yes, I can do that," Jill says.

"I'd also like to task you with some bigger projects that will let you show some of your skills at a higher level. How does that sound?"

Jill is visibly relieved. "Yes, that is exciting. Thank you!"

"Is there anything else you want to talk about?"

"Yes," Jill requests. "I'd like to ask for consideration when others don't get their segments of the project done so that I can do mine."

"I see. Let me think about that and see if I can come up with a solution we can all work with to keep the workflow process smooth," Kira says. "I'll get back to you by the end of the week — does that work?"

"Yes, thank you." Jill is smiling at this point and leaves Kira's office feeling relieved.

Solving & Moving

Clearly, the second scenario is much more effective for a multitude of reasons. The biggest difference between the two co-workers is that Kira has actively enlisted Jill in thinking about what she can do in the future and is making her expectations and requests clear. She has prevented Jill's brain from going into the past — conjuring up defenses and focusing on reasons and excuses for her past mistakes.

Instead, she is using her time and energy focusing Jill on what she and the business need moving forward. Kira is curious and is listening, asking for alignment, and owning her role in the disconnect

— whether she agrees with that perception or not. She spends only a short time acknowledging the past and the majority of the time enlisting and connecting Jill into the future expectation. With these requests, she is also able to put Jill's mind into an opportunity-focused environment where she can stop the negative behavior and step up to focus on what she really wants.

As leaders, a primary part of our job is to solve problems and move the team forward. In the early part of my career, I was rewarded for speed. The quicker I could deal with something, the smaller the subsequent problem would be. I was in a reactive state almost all of the time. The restaurant business requires 24/7 oversight, especially when the team is small, homegrown, and unsure of what lies ahead.

The problem with being in a constant reactive state is, we are often out of control emotionally and our fight or flight response kicks in — driving negative behavior patterns. Rather than recognizing a need for a pause, we often behave in a way that is out of alignment with our values, and we aren't able to access clear thought processes. We have all woken up the next morning with a pit in our stomach as the dust clears and we wish we could rewind. I've learned that waiting until I can get in a space to respond versus react will almost always allow me to practice the Windshield Theory and create a forward-focused strategy with more positive results.

The Windshield Theory also applies to our personal growth stories and internal narratives. We are often our own worst critics, and our failures inform the risks we have the opportunity to take, the innovations we create, and ultimately the life path we travel. As we age, we learn more slowly because we know all of the mistakes that we have made in the past and have become skilled in preventing them or avoiding risks around them.

It's human nature to protect ourselves, avoid danger, and prevent pain. However, if we can quantify the worst thing that can happen while taking a risk and then deciding whether we can live with that, it's much easier to take the plunge. For me, it takes the Windshield

Theory to take the risk and then ultimately handle the consequence or optimize the reward.

An internal narrative example:

Joe attends a speech given by John Mackey, the Founder of Whole Foods, who was someone he had looked up to for many years and had wanted to meet for a long time. He arrives early and sits in the front row, waiting to glean whatever information he can from this exceptional leader. John's speech is even more inspiring than Joe could have imagined. Afterward, when John is having his microphone removed, Joe is faced with a choice.

Choice A:

Joe sits in his chair, studying John, wondering if John would be all right with an audience member approaching him. He looks busy. John pulls his phone out of his pocket and checks the time.

Joe thinks to himself, "See, he probably has to go. He's so busy, and everyone wants something from him. Even if I talk to him, what is that going to do? He probably gets a million requests from people and finds it really annoying."

Joe packs his backpack up as he watches others approach John, and then Joe walks out of the conference center.

Choice B:

Identifying the risk he's presented with, Joe's belly churns. He quickly thinks to himself, "What is my loss here? Getting told, 'You have to go!' by John Mackey? I can handle that." He smiles.

He rushes to be the first person to greet John, who is pulling the mic cord out of his sweater.

"Hey, John! I am a huge fan and wanted to say hello!" Joe says excitedly. "I really connected with your story early on in my career, particularly the work you have done with Conscious Capitalism." He adds, "In fact, I developed some software to help companies systematize their work around these efforts."

John replies, "Really, that's cool! What is it called? We have always had a hard time with the system side of the effort."

There is a young woman standing behind Joe who seems like she wants to say hello as well.

Joe says, "It looks like there are a lot of folks here who want to meet you too." He asks, "Do you have a card so that I can send you some more information?"

John reaches into his pocket and hands his card to Joe. "Sure, that would be great. Thanks for coming by." He smiles.

Joe is beaming ear to ear, practically sprinting out of that conference center. He will later go on to partner with and receive funding from John to grow his own business.

Deeper Connection
(The 6 Primary Behaviors of the Windshield Theory)

What I have learned over the years is that the most successful people get really good at taking risks and putting themselves out there. They use that risk-taking to create constant momentum that propels their next step up. They are obsessed with building their community (I like this word better than networking) because they learn that this is what drives businesses and people forward. Faster than anything. Keeping yourself in forward motion is absolutely critical to growth — personally and professionally.

In closing, I want you to consider the 6 Primary Behaviors of the Windshield Theory:

1. Curiosity
2. Radical Ownership
3. Knowledge of the Past, Focus on the Future

4. A Strong Relationship with Risk
5. Respond, Don't React
6. A Positive Belief System

Training my brain to be in forward motion with my personal narrative, interpersonal interactions, and leadership has had a tremendously positive effect on all things in my life. It's given me the gift of knowing I can take control of my outcomes and have a bigger impact, and that my opportunities are limitless. I have seen transformational development with my leaders and a deeper connection within our team. I will always choose to see the road ahead!

4TH QUARTER

As we enter the fourth quarter of our lives, we're hitting it around 55 years old. We've invested so much time in our future and ourselves. We've had great mentors who invested their time, money, and resources in us. And, ideally, we've had at least one coach who helped us reach the next level so that we could see how we needed to further invest in ourselves.

Some of us may have started families. And for those who have done so, some may already have grandkids. No matter the case, we're beginning to look at our generational wealth in some capacity — be it for our family, community, or future generations in need. The fourth quarter is when it's time to look at your career and start finalizing the outlook for the last 10 to 30 years — or for those who are lucky, maybe 45 years — that we have left.

We've worked so hard. We've received our education. We've changed jobs anywhere from three to eight times. We've evolved in our true calling, our perfect career. We're approaching the stage in which we can officially retire. Some of us may have already gotten some really nice breaks. Some of us have been making or looking into making the right investments for our future. Others have even sold a big company and retired early.

Professional athletes often retire from their sports by age 40. And those who were very smart with their money can live the rest of their life in the clear, financially. Some of them may have another five to ten years left to continue playing in order to fully set themselves up for their final Overtime.

For the rest of us, you're working through your 50s; you're setting up for retirement by 70. Your investment is shifting in a slightly different direction. Instead of continuing to invest in yourself in order to find a new job, or your true career, your investment is now shifting to the future. You are now beginning to visualize your retirement. You are now seeing how you can further build upon the investments you made into yourself over the first three quarters, which have financially put you in a great position.

The total of your investments over the course of these four quarters will provide the means for accomplishing your bucket list. What do you want that to look like? Is it traveling? Is it visiting family and friends around the country — or the world? Is it finally writing that book you've had in your imagination all these years? Is it setting up nonprofits or charities? Does your true calling go beyond that final round of clocking out? What might that look like?

Just as others helped you see how you are a number one asset, I believe it's inevitably your turn to show others how they are as well. This could be your family's next generation, and it could be your community. If you aren't already finding opportunities to pay it forward, now is the time to begin discovering them.

While you continue working hard in your passion, spend time on your retirement goals. Not only will doing this motivate you, it will give you a plan that you can put into action when you officially step out of your career. Also, take advantage of the part where there's no scoreboard. Enjoy this last round. The game is still on!

ABOUT ELAINA VERHOFF

 Elaina Verhoff is the founder of Elaina V. Public Relations, a boutique public relations agency located in Phoenix, Arizona. With 25-plus years of communications expertise, she has helped small startups to Fortune 100 companies craft their message, build their brand, and increase their business. Through her years working in public relations, she has established close media relationships that help her gain local and national media coverage, win prestigious awards, and gain recognition for clients.

10

RISK BEFORE THE OTHER SIDE

by
Elaina Verhoff

I was raised to follow the expected path. Get a four-year degree. Find a stable job with benefits. Avoid risk at all costs. And that was just fine with me. I was a studious kid and a rule follower.

My journals may have been filled with visions of the bed-and-breakfast/bookstore I envisioned running someday. But I took my parents' guidance to heart, got a degree in political science, then followed in the steps of my father and grandfather and jumped into the world of PR.

After working at PR agencies for a few years, I again got the entrepreneurial itch and decided to apply to business school — with the intention of learning how to be an entrepreneur and THEN starting my own business. I quickly learned that business school was not focused on entrepreneurship but structured to churn out freshly minted MBAs ready for lucrative careers in the corporate world.

When I saw the starting salaries and signing bonuses that were being doled out, I quickly shifted my path and got ready to hop on the corporate ladder. A summer internship led to a coveted position with a major automotive company that paid very well, took me to Laguna Beach, and enabled me to work at the corporate headquarters of multiple car companies. Life was good. Stressful, but good.

After getting married, becoming a mom, and missing out on way too many firsts with my baby, then toddler, I decided the time had come to take a break from the corporate world and become a full-time mom. I dedicated several years to raising my kids and finding my creative outlet through freelance writing and blogging. As the kids got older, I got back into PR, taking a job at a local PR agency where I was soon managing a number of the firm's biggest accounts and supervising junior staff. But through it all, deep down, I still had a desire to create something of my own.

Take the Risk

I'll never forget the moment I quit my job. Circumstances had been leading up to it for some time, and when the breaking point arrived, I felt a quiet calm come over me as I told my boss I would be leaving. Did I have a plan? No. Did I have clients lined up and ready to go? Nope. Insurance? Nah. But what I did have was a feeling in my gut that I was doing the right thing, and everything would fall into place.

Someone asked me the other day, "How did you do it? How did you have the confidence to leave a stable job and start your own company?" I told them that I was fortunate to have had two people in my life who specifically gave me the extra push I needed to follow my gut. The first was a close friend. He knew I was unhappy and was about to make a decision to take another job or go out on my own. He was the voice in my ear telling me to take a chance and go for it. If it didn't work out, I could always get a job. But if it did, a whole new world would open up to me. He would joke about taking the "red pill" and never going back, and while I didn't appreciate the full meaning at the time, I certainly do now.

I also invited a longtime friend of my parents to lunch for some advice. He had owned his own PR agency for decades, so I wanted to ask him — based on his experience, would he advise me to take the safe route or strike out on my own? I expected him to tell me to stick with safe, steady employment. I was dead wrong. He said he himself had zero regrets, that I had a great reputation in the business, and he knew I would be a success. It's funny how sometimes other people believe in us more than we do ourselves. That's the last time I will make that mistake.

After denying my entrepreneurial itch for decades, I knew the time had come.

In a way, I feel like those of us who have made the choice to believe in and invest in ourselves owe it to others to encourage them to do the same. Having gone through the startup phase of slow growth — during a pandemic, no less — followed by success, it feels like I've earned a badge of honor by going through the tunnel and emerging on the other side. And I want others to know that they can do the same.

I had a conversation yesterday with a woman who told me her job was "sucking the soul out of her." And, from prior experience, I could relate. To everyone who feels like they are in a situation where they aren't feeling happy or fulfilled, or worse, that they are living a groundhog day-like existence, I say this: You have one life. You will know when you hit the point where you are ready to make a change … to follow a new path that will leave you waking up excited for what lies ahead. If you are good at something and enjoy doing it, you may not have a business plan or clients lined up to work with you. But if you have a passion and a talent, those are the very basic elements needed to get started.

Start small. Be patient. With time and small successes, your endeavor will grow. Word will spread, and you will attract like-minded people who want to work with you. Approach this new beginning with the spirit of wanting to help others, and know that small wins lead to big wins. For me, it truly has been a snowball effect. And I have given myself permission to try new things, to fail, to learn, and to move forward again. I do more of what works, less of what doesn't. And I enjoy the process.

I don't think I could ever go back to working for someone else. It's absolutely invigorating to choose how and where I will spend my days and who I will work with. My joy has increased exponentially, and I want to be the spark that inspires others to experience the same.

Recommendations from the Other Side!

In the spirit of encouraging others to pursue their purpose and follow their own entrepreneurial path, I have a few suggestions. I have confidence that anyone who has talent and passion can succeed and live a life that far surpasses what they even dreamed was possible. Just remember, be patient and be consistent, and success will come. Here goes!

Leap before you're ready

Some of us are natural born entrepreneurs. Some of us aren't. I now realize that this doesn't matter. I was in my 40s when I started my first company, so I truly believe that it's never too late. I'm here to tell you: if I can do it, you can do it.

Celebrate successes

Social media is a completely free way to get exposure for who you are and what you are doing. Create social media accounts and share your successes. Announce the launch of your company. Celebrate your clients and your wins publicly. Use your social accounts to promote others too and — guess what — the love and attention will come right back to you.

Use PR to spread the word

Public relations or earned media is the perfect way to bring awareness and attention to who you are and what you're doing. Write a press release announcing your new company. Have a great photo taken. Send your announcement and photo to editors of publications your target clients read.

Are you an expert in a particular area? Find a newsworthy angle and reach out to local TV and radio stations, newspapers, and digital outlets and offer yourself up for interviews. Look for the articles, interviews, and features on others that you want to be featured in and do the research to find out who to contact to pitch yourself for the same coverage.

This happens to be my specialty, so I invite you to learn more and reach out to me (www.alwaysaheadseries.com).

ABOUT LaDARREN LANDRUM

LaDarren Landrum is a performance coach based in Phoenix, Arizona. He serves his community by championing healthy lifestyles for anyone and everyone he makes contact with. He is a husband as well as a father to three beautiful little girls.

Since concluding his obligated time and being honorably discharged from the Marine Corps, he is looking to possibly step into another uniform as a first responder (firefighter). Simultaneously, he is taking steps toward opening his own fitness club in the Phoenix metro area. LaDarren also has his own fitness lifestyle clothing brand called FIT-IN Athletics, in which he coins inspirational quotes and phrases and slaps them on apparel to serve as daily reminders to maintain a progressive mindset on whatever journey an individual sets forth on.

LaDarren wholeheartedly believes that fitness (mental and physical) is a vehicle that anyone and everyone can and should drive on whatever road they decide to take to get to wherever they're going.

Most people live believable lives and accomplish believable things. When you set out on your journey, promise yourself to see it all the way through and have no problem crashing or burning on the way. Set out to live an unbelievable life and accomplish unbelievable things.

11

KILLING DOUBTS FOR A LIVING

by
LaDarren Landrum

I was born and raised in Spartanburg, South Carolina — a product of a single-father household. The fact that I had my father in my life made me an anomaly in my neighborhood, seeing as most of the kids I grew up around did not know theirs. After being bullied in the schoolyard, I was led to the art of boxing. I participated in three amateur Golden Gloves boxing championships. After that, and many failed attempts at team sports, I graduated from high school with a 3.4 GPA, only to get to college and flunk out after my freshman year.

My grades dropping meant losing my scholarship and having to drop out of college. It was back to my childhood home. We made a deal, my father and I — a written, signed, and even laminated deal — that I would pay my way. "That is what being a man is all about," my father said. He and I came up with a number that made sense. And that is what I paid monthly. Outside of those monthly dues for my stay in my father's house, I was only responsible for my phone bill.

Apart from my dues, any other money that I could scrape together was going toward a Nissan Titan pickup truck that I had had my eyes on. There was nothing I wanted more than that truck. My father was well aware of my goal to purchase this, as well as our agreed-upon monthly total. In fact, he had a bunch of laminated papers posted around the house to remind me of my dues.

For some reason, he was asking for money beyond our agreement. I didn't understand why. And quite frankly, it upset me, because we had a deal, and that was being breached. This minor disagreement grew into a major verbal altercation that was dancing on a fine line — the other side of which was physical.

I've always had the utmost respect for my father. He raised me pretty much on his own. So he was the only person I ever really had. That said, this disagreement made me feel like I couldn't trust him anymore. The man who chewed me out when I brought home a B grade. The man who lectured me about composure and keeping a cool head. The man who taught me about the importance of embracing my individuality and marking my own path. The man who never gave up on me. If I couldn't trust him, I couldn't trust anyone.

Being homeless did not just happen to me. I wasn't forced to leave my father's house. And I had plenty of other places to go. But the truth is, none of those options felt like a place where I would feel safe. They were homes of people who, through no fault of their own, I couldn't trust. I couldn't trust my own father. No. Being homeless was a conscious decision, and it was arguably the best one I ever made. I walked away from my father's house one day, the only home I'd ever known. And I never looked back.

I found myself homeless at 19 years old — cold, wet, and alone — sleeping on a park bench. During my time on the street, between working dead-end gigs, countless odd jobs, and attending community college, I really honed in on my physical fitness more than ever before. Even before this time of my life, I'd always felt like I was missing something. This felt more true than ever.

My Body as a Weapon

Sleeping on a bench in Cleveland Park in Spartanburg, South Carolina, no matter how high the sun was or how bright the day was, it was always dark. I always found myself on a hamster wheel of dark, negative thoughts. These thoughts are the reason I believe that most people in similar circumstances turn to drug addiction and alcohol abuse — or worst case, even suicide. I'd never even thought of trying any of those options. And I did not want to start.

All I could think to do was to drop and do push-ups until my arms started to hurt. My thought was that by doing so, pushing up until I felt the burn would take my mind off all the negativity that was taking up too much real estate in my mind. It worked. From that moment forward, if I wasn't working a double shift at the local family favorite, Wade's Restaurant, delivering furniture for Mattress Maxx, hosting karaoke and dance night for Wigging Out Entertainment, or going to class, I was training. Even to get to a gig, I walked, ran, or biked, so technically I was always training.

I made up my mind to turn my body into a weapon to kill any doubt that I ever had in myself. I replaced negative thoughts with disciplined action. And once again, I never looked back.

There are three philosophies that I learned on the street, and I still hold them true today:

1. If you have to pick a vice, pick a progressive one
2. FIT IN
3. First it hurts, then it changes you

#1: If you have to pick a vice, pick a progressive one

Again, I decided to roll over and do push-ups until my arms hurt. In the face of negative thoughts, this was a progressive vice. And the great thing about a push-up is that it's a very foundational strength movement, and the only equipment you need is yourself and your will to push. Literally, all you need to do is push yourself. It's that simple.

#2: FIT IN

This is an acronym that I developed to serve as a plan of action moving forward. It later turned into a brand name for my performance coaching business. Character is not a product of circumstance — it is what survives despite it.

FIT IN:

★ **F** orm a vision
★ **I** nitiate contact with your goals
★ **T** rain hard
★ **I** nspire others
★ **N** ever quit

#3: First it hurts, then it changes you

For better or worse, it's up to you. I embraced the pain I was immersed in. I chose the positive outlet of fitness, and it opened so many doors for me. I made it through serving my country and three Olympic campaigns — need I say more?

What Are You Waiting On?

My fitness not only gave me a positive outlet from the traumas of living on the street, it also led me to the United States Marine

Corps. Twenty-six days into being on the street, I was approached at school, on my way to the library, by a Marine Corps recruiter. But Staff Sergeant Stewart didn't talk to me about joining the corps. He asked me to be his training partner, specifically for his long-distance runs. We committed to running twice a week together.

Up to this point, someone to train with and push me was not something I'd had before. It made me feel like I was a part of something important. Up until that point, I'd never felt a part of anything. It was six weeks of nonstop training, which included lifting three times a week at the local YMCA and trail running twice a week with my recruiter. I was also riding my one-speed beach cruiser to and from gigs, to and from school, and everywhere else in between.

Staff Sergeant Stewart had me take the Marine Corps initial strength test (IST), which is used in recruitment to determine your physical readiness to become a marine. The IST tests your maximum amount of pull-ups, your maximum amount of sit-ups in a two-minute time stamp, and a timed 1.5 mile run in which you run as fast as you can. Based on the outcome of my IST, the question finally made his way into my head:

What are you waiting on?

The way I saw it, I was 19 and living on the street. I didn't have a home. I wasn't close to my family. It would be better that I be the one taking the weight of combat, the possibility of going to war, than a 19-year-old who *did* have a home and *was* close to their family. And so, I committed to eight years in the Marine Corps.

As I was getting started, I was told by one of my instructors that at some point in my career, my physical fitness would determine whether I lived or died. Well, unknown to him, I had already embraced just that while I was on the street. The discipline it took to train when I did not feel like it set me free from the bad things that negative thoughts could have led me to. Pushing myself and instilling in my mind that I would not be a victim of negativity ensured my survival on the street and catapulted me into my Marine Corps career.

Negative thoughts, such as self-doubt, grab hold of the best of us. And they hold on for dear life. We can't control whether negative thoughts make their way into our mental Rolodex. But we can control how long they stay there and in which direction they make us move.

Excuses have sort of a negative connotation attached to them. But the truth is, we all have them. What separates us is whether we use them to give up or to keep going. You need to mentally transcend where you are first. And your body? That'll follow. Mine did.

Nevertheless, here are three philosophies I learned in the Marine Corps that I still hold true today:

1. Your physical fitness at some point will determine whether you live or die.
2. It costs too much to be lazy.
3. Slow is smooth. Smooth is fast.

#1: Your physical fitness at some point will determine whether you live or die.

As I could immediately agree, my instructor was correct. This is not only true in places of war and combat, it's also true in everyday civilian life. Even if you develop a chronic illness — such as heart disease, the main one here in the U.S. — hereditarily or just through poor lifestyle choices, being physically fit reduces the chance of it beating you in the long run.

#2: It costs too much to be lazy.

Being lazy can cost you time, money, and, in extreme cases, your life or the life of someone you love dearly. That's serious. It costs too damn much to be lazy.

#3: Slow is smooth. Smooth is fast.

There's nothing learned through a rushed process. Embracing every step of the process gives you lifelong skills and wisdom that cannot be taken from you or exploited. Take your time. Learn. Develop.

Cardio Blessings

Not even halfway through my Marine Corps contract, physical fitness ensured my survival in combat. Not only that, as shared, it also led me to training and competing at the U.S. Olympic level for three different sports and division 1 collegiate level for another. And in October of 2022, my time as an obligated marine ended — but not my time as a serviceman.

In fact, previously, in 2017 a fellow veteran and myself started an official 501(c)(3) nonprofit to help our homeless brothers and sisters get off the streets. We started this while we were both still in service, due to an unfortunate circumstance.

My buddy, a former Army Airborne infantryman, was crippled by a series of back surgeries due to service-related injuries. After a life of being active, he was confined to using a walker to get around and was prone to collapsing after a simple sneeze. Naturally, he slipped into extreme depression.

After some encouraging words from me, he made up his mind to start walking daily to regain his strength. As time went on, he graduated to walking with weight on his back again. The weight he chose to carry was jars of peanut butter, loaves of bread, and bottled water to hand out to the less fortunate whom he came across on his route. One day, he decided to document his act of service, going live on Facebook with a small audience, including me, watching. He spoke to his stream, saying he was blessing people while getting his cardio in.

And so, Cardio Blessings, Incorporated, was born.

It became a four-boot, two-man operation from that moment forward. Each month following, the both of us would hike around different cities with our rucksacks filled with food, water, and supplies for the less fortunate. We received national news attention. More importantly, we made a difference. And we're not finished by a long shot.

During the remainder of my time serving my country, and still to this very day, I served my community through Cardio Blessings. Today, as a husband and father, I also serve my community as a performance coach. I call it "killing doubts for a living." I help people overcome mental and physical barriers preventing their progress by introducing optimal movement and quality exercise into their daily lives.

Outside expanding the reach of Cardio Blessings, my short-term goal is to open my own fitness club here in the Phoenix metro area. I've also danced with the idea of becoming a fireman. The truth is, I can see myself doing it all simultaneously. So, stand by.

ABOUT RICK LaRUE

 If you ask Rick what he does, he will say, "I love life." His two children and their families bring him unmitigated joy and inspiration. He and his wife, Sandy, have been married for 46 years, many of which were spent apart because of work travel. Now they enjoy nearly every hour of every day together. Want to stack the odds in your favor for a healthy marriage? Trust each other, respect each other, and communicate!

Rick works with select clients who are seeking personal and professional guidance. With a focus on balance and inner peace, he guides them through a series of agreed-upon objectives, which brings contentment to a point of clarity and essence. This, in turn, modifies behavior that will be directed toward happiness and overall fulfillment. The goal is to create acute self-awareness within people so that they may begin the journey of setting realistic objectives, learning what success feels like, and gaining an insight toward a state of enhanced balance in their lives.

Rick is also the owner of Export and Grow, which is a company that connects manufacturers of quality foods with retailers, distributors, and agents on a global scale. Leveraging the equity of industry knowledge, trustworthy contacts, and 40 years of building a reputation as a man of utmost integrity, he is harvesting what he spent years planting.

12

TO THE HOLY GRAIL (BELIEVE IN YOUR OWN SUCCESS STORY)

by

Rick LaRue

Everyone has their own perception and valuation of the word "success" when it comes to personal reconciliation.

I was conceived and delivered from parents who …

- Never loved each other
- Never uttered the words "I love you" to any of their three children
- Never fostered harmony, family values, individual growth, morals, ethics, formal education, or collaboration of any sort

My father was a truck driver, when he was so inclined to work. He never had a steady job but instead played cards and gambled two to three nights a week and on weekends. He was never home. My mother worked at an envelope factory, and she was also in various bands that played gigs on Friday and Saturday evenings. My father was 20 years older than my mother, and my mother was 19 years old when she had me. The math states that I was conceived well before they were married. My parents hated each other and blamed each other and their three children for the pitiful lives that they led.

Via heartbreak, personal observation, awareness, education, and collaboration, I was able to discern what was dysfunctional and knew that I wanted to be a better person than what the circumstantial situation had handed me. I overcame poverty, a lack of parental guidance, being frustrated and angry as a young adult, homelessness, business failures, and a negative perspective about the world around myself. And I did so through a series of cognizant choices that led to personal growth and development at a relatively young age.

We lived on the second floor of a three-decker apartment in New England. One day when I was seven years old, I returned home from school and saw that the front gate to the house was blocked. There was a sign on the house and on the gate that stated this in large bold letters:

CONDEMNED!
Unfit for Human Habitation
Worcester Department of Public Health and Welfare

We stayed with a neighbor for a week until the house was repaired to the bare minimum for us to live in. I was tormented daily by neighborhood kids for being in such a situation. From that day forward, I was determined to always have money.

So, from the time that I was ten years old, I had paper routes. The kind where you find scrap wood, build a wagon with wheels that you purchased from the Salvation Army, go to various street corners, pick up your bundles of newspapers, and begin delivering — in the rain, snow, cold, or heat. I had a morning route, an evening route, and a Sunday paper route — roughly 300 customers in all, and people depended on me. I had responsibilities and people paid me to be accountable. I saved my money, and my spending habits were very judicious. I provided myself with personal comforts with the money that I earned.

When I was 15 years old, I met the woman who is now my wife of 46 years. Why her? I saw that she was the exact opposite of me, and I needed her kind of positive energy in my life. She was the good girl, from a great family environment. Loving, supportive, compassionate, intelligent, honest, a person of faith, and driven to be the best that she could be across all domains. I was the bad boy, and together we became a team, with amazing collective emotional and intellectual personal resources and bountiful synergies. We helped each other improve and continue to do so every day.

Most of the guys I grew up with had older brothers who couldn't wait until they were 16 years old so that they could quit school. When I turned 16, I moved out of the house and lived in a room with a bunk and a nightstand at a truck stop for a while. I worked at the truck stop, pumping fuel and doing everything from selling flowers to shoveling snow to earn money for tuition and basic subsistence. I had the opportunity to listen to many truck drivers tell me what they should have done differently in their respective lives. That invaluable opportunity to observe and listen to so many people from so many different backgrounds provided me with a much broader scope and vision about people, places, and things than I had ever imagined. I developed a thirst to understand myself and my relationship with life.

When I was 18 years old, I lived in the back of my pickup truck at a state park for roughly half of my high school senior year. There was a man by the name of Cal Green who lived in a tan Buick station wagon next to me. He was an unambitious sage — a man of profound wisdom and no desire to improve himself. The lesson:

WISDOM WITHOUT AMBITION, DRIVE, AND GOAL ORIENTATION IS USELESS WHEN IT COMES TO CREATING THE OPPORTUNITY TO ENJOY PHYSICAL AND MENTAL COMFORTS.

After I graduated from high school, over the next two-plus years, I hitchhiked across the U.S. three times, and traversed it twice on a Harley-Davidson. It was the '70s, and I was free to be me. Greatest lesson learned:

WATER SEEKS ITS OWN LEVEL.

One hitchhiking trip began in Worcester, Massachusetts, with a destination of Yosemite National Park, California. My friend and I were clean, neat in appearance, and overall well-kept because we believed that we would get rides quicker than people who looked disheveled. On the very same entrance ramp as us were two hippies who had the same destination.

We thought that because of their appearance they would rot to death before reaching Yosemite. Unbelievably, three days later, we ran into them at Tuolumne Meadows campground in Yosemite and learned that we had arrived within a few hours of one another. We had had great rides from clean-cut people, while they had traversed from van to van with their own kind all the way to California. The lesson:

THESE PEOPLE ARE MY PEERS. (SEEK AND ALIGN MYSELF WITH PEOPLE WHO ARE GOOD AT HEART, SMART, DRIVEN, AND GOAL-ORIENTED.)

After traveling the country, and about two dozen jobs between the ages of 18 and 20, I was ready for life. A different life. A life with real goals, contrived from real choices that would bear real consequences.

First and foremost, I needed to get a college education, and I had no money for tuition. I also wanted to explore Europe. I joined the United States Air Force in 1975 because they offered the GI bill — a conduit to a tuition-free college degree, perhaps world travel, and a sorely needed platform for becoming a responsible adult.

My first duty station assignment was in Clovis, New Mexico, and it offered no opportunities toward education or Europe, so I created my own. After being on base for about six months, I learned that one of the men in my squadron was married to the Officer in Charge of Base Personnel. He and I would have brief conversational exchanges when passing each other in the hallway or in a meeting room.

Over time, I asked him several questions about his personal life and put together a mental profile of what his wife was like. I shared my ambitions with him, and asked if he would facilitate a meeting with his wife, and he obliged. I went to the Personnel Office, introduced myself to the Officer in Charge, and appealed to her compassionate side in a conversation that conveyed that my biggest goal in life was to go to college, and if possible, in Europe.

She was a strong proponent of education. She confided that during her career she had heard this story hundreds of times, from hundreds of people who had never capitalized on the opportunity to earn a college degree while in the military. I told her that I was serious and would enroll in two classes at Eastern New Mexico University to prove it.

I enrolled, got good grades, and proudly returned to the Personnel Officer with my grades. About four months later, I received orders to go to Italy. My extended five-year tour of duty yielded a BA in English and Psychology from the University of Maryland Global Campus, and I was just shy of my Masters in Business Management — which I completed when I returned to the United States. No small task, considering that I had my full-time job in the military and a family.

I went to school five nights per week and every Saturday morning, for nearly five years. Between semesters, my wife and I captured the opportunity to see the greater part of Europe. Albeit from various campgrounds, the history that we learned, the beautiful landscapes that we saw, and the cultural nuances that we experienced were the same as if we had stayed at a five-star hotel. The lesson:

SEEK OUT PEOPLE WHOM YOU CAN COLLABORATE WITH, AND CREATE WIN-WIN SITUATIONS.

Plato is credited with the adage "Necessity is the mother of invention." This is my mantra, and I espouse it frequently to myself. Believe deeply in yourself beyond any perceived limitations, and you will discover that you are a force to be reckoned with. Life isn't a sprint. It is a marathon! You need to train yourself to pack your own lunch, carve your own destiny, ride the peaks, tough out the valleys, find inner strength through peace, do your absolute best to never compromise your values, and all the while stay focused on your goals.

It strikes different people in different ways and at different times, but there is always that one day that you wake up, look in the mirror, and you formulate strong, stark, unmitigated sentiments about your physical, mental, and emotional well-being. If you have not already done so, DO IT! Take your purest, most candid thoughts and observations seriously, incubate ideas for self-improvement, formulate attainable action plans that will yield the results that you are seeking, and begin. The lesson:

MAKE DEFINITIVE CHOICES, AND EXECUTE!

Where does it get sticky? Perception and control.

PERCEPTION: I can never experience your perceptions, nor can you ever experience mine. We all see situations from entirely different multifaceted points of view. Is the glass half empty, or half full? That depends upon how YOU look at it and how you perceive the level of content. Perception can drive you to deep despair or elevate you to a feeling of euphoria that may be perceived as a false sense of success to another. The lesson:

YOU NEED YOUR OWN GAME PLAN TO ACHIEVE WHAT YOU BELIEVE TO BE YOUR OWN SUCCESS STORY.

It is your life, and you need to contrive your own path by making choices that will bear fruit.

CONTROL: You need to structure yourself to be in control of your boundaries, learn how to handle challenges, and decide how to parcel your energies in order to achieve your goals. Gauge your limits, your risk tolerance, your assets, your strengths, and your perceived weaknesses, and understand that a beautiful life isn't always accomplished by coloring within the lines. The lesson:

STAY FOCUSED ON THE GOAL, AND ADJUST AS NECESSARY ALONG THE WAY!

After six years in the military, I was much better prepared to experience success in life. At that time, my wife and I had two children, aged five and three. Unemployment was over 11 percent, mortgage rates were in the 17 percent range, and finding work was very difficult. I found employment in the accounting department at a company that was constructing a highly controversial nuclear power plant.

The job was terrible, but I started side gigs such as a van transportation service to and from work for colleagues in my department who lived close to one another. On weekends I used the van to organize trips to sporting events. I made money on the tickets, the beer, the food, and of course, the transportation.

When I left the accounting department, I started a delicatessen with one of my colleagues from the department. He convinced me that he knew all about the deli business. He didn't.

I crafted a plan that allowed us to own 75 percent of the business when we opened, with 25 percent belonging to investors. Unknowingly, the investors paid the entire 100 percent for us to be able to open with no debt. The business grew to two delicatessens and a bakery. We were wholesaling products that we baked, and from the outside, business looked great. I was the "outside" guy doing the sales and distribution of items that we made, and my partner was the "inside" guy.

He was robbing me blind. Through a series of events, the business failed. On my 30th birthday, I was cleaning out the building as the bank's hired hands repossessed the furnishings. I was $40,000 in business debt and $20,000 in credit card debt — with not a penny in the bank. I lived in government-subsidized housing and felt like I was failing my family.

Within days of the closure, I got a job as a substitute English teacher at a high school in Epping, New Hampshire, because a teacher was beginning her pregnancy leave. Shortly thereafter, a woman who used to eat lunch at the deli called me and told me that the company that her husband worked at was hiring. It was a corporate sales job, THE HOLY GRAIL! I competed against roughly 325 people for the position and was selected for the job. Over time, I paid whomever I owed money to from past experiences. After 11 years of corporate America, I had climbed the ladder from Territory Representative in the Boston area to a position that had national and international reach, but I wanted something different — something that I would have a hand in crafting. I took on a sales position with a small family-owned confectionery business in Baltimore that had been around for 94 years. It was perfect.

About six months into the stint, I was eager to make more money. An opportunity presented itself, and the outcome was that one of the family members and I restructured one of their side businesses. He owned 50.666 percent of the business, and I owned 49.333 percent. My buy-in was $7,000 to cover a portion of the existing debt, and in the first year, I made $29,000 on that investment.

The business produced over $1 million in revenue for each one of us over the next few years. I bought a very nice sailboat and some real estate with my earnings. I eventually sold my share of the company back to the original owner for the $7,000 that I had paid for it. Yes, it was worth more, but I was extremely grateful for the opportunity to be able to put my children through college, live in a nice home, and enjoy the rest of my life. To me, that was priceless!

I retired at 50 years old, started a business with my son shortly thereafter, and eventually was recruited and hired by the fourth largest cookie company in the world to sell and distribute products in the U.S. and all of the Walmart and Sam's Club locations globally. That segued into a position of VP of International Sales for the largest manufacturer of fruit snacks in the world, from where I eventually retired again at the age of 66.

I never doubted that I would be a highly resourceful, well-traveled, well-educated man of integrity and ingenuity, a good husband, a good father, a good provider, a good employee, a good employer, a good teacher, and above all a happy and comfortable man. In my career, I was able to travel to all 50 states (many of them several times) and visit 63 countries first-class. Why? Because I BELIEVED IN MYSELF! I created my own vision, developed and executed my own plans, stayed true to myself, honored my core beliefs, accepted my consequences, and never lost sight of the prize … a comfortable life.

Remember the lessons:

- Wisdom without ambition is useless.
- Water seeks its own level. Seek and align yourself with people whom you admire and respect because of their goodness, intellect, and goal orientation.

- Seek out people to engage with in win-win collaborations.
- Make definitive choices and execute!
- You need your own game plan to achieve what you believe to be your own success story.
- Stay focused on the goal and adjust as necessary along the way.
- Believe in yourself.

Know who you are and who you want to be. Be the architect and builder of your life. Understand the roots of your perceptions, and create roads to your belief of success. It's your life.

CONCLUSION

Thank you so much for reading this anthology of amazing stories. I wanted to share 12 different people from 12 different backgrounds coming up with different ways of defining success in their life. Along the way, important people and mentors invested in their journey, or they invested in themselves as well as generations to come. In all cases, no matter the challenge, they were willing and able to overcome obstacles and create fulfilling futures for themselves and their families. I hope you're inspired to do the same, no matter which quarter of life you're in at this moment.

As a reminder, for the purposes of this book, I've broken down the quarters of life as follows.

1st Quarter (Age 0–21)
- Our childhood years through graduating college (most likely in our early 20s).
- Our family, community, and educational staff have invested in our future as a number one asset.

2nd Quarter (Age 22–40)

- Our formative years, stepping into the world to explore our career.
- Over the course of multiple jobs and roles, we get closer and closer to our true calling (which will one day become our career).
- Employers and mentors invest time and knowledge (and maybe finances) into helping us grow as professionals.
- By the time we hit our 40s, ideally we understand for ourselves that we are a number one asset and how we can continue our evolution.

3rd Quarter (Age 41–55)

- Our mature years, stepping further into our path and our true calling.
- Over the course of conferences and networking events, we are meeting and hiring professional coaches to help us level up our skills and mindset.
- Our wealth is beginning to accrue and we are setting up for the final quarter beyond our 50s!

4th Quarter (Age 56–70)

- As we continue investing in ourselves, we are also finding opportunities to invest in future generations (family, nonprofits, philanthropism, etc.).
- As we are approaching retirement, we are finding opportunities to rest and restore ourselves.
- We are focusing on clarifying and solidifying our vision of life beyond our 70s.
- Our wealth is the highest it's ever been and is protected against uncertainty.

No matter which quarter you might be in, I hope this book is enlightening. As you read about ideas and life challenges similar to your own, I hope you're realizing that you aren't alone on an island. Whether you're ahead of some or catching up to others, there are many beside you at this very moment.

The four quarters cover years and change, which can be daunting, but all roads lead to Overtime. Ideally, this is when you no longer have to work — and you have saved enough generational wealth for you and future generations in your family legacy. This is the purpose of the book! If you invest early in yourself — and find mentors who are willing to invest in you — you can hit Overtime at any moment or age.

In Overtime, you should be spending as much time every day doing things that you love …

- Spending time with your children or grandchildren
- Volunteering
- Mentoring
- Sharing your knowledge with the next generation
- Luxuriating
- Enjoying your empire
- Traveling the world (by yourself or with someone who melts your heart)

That is the purpose of investing early in yourself. You're betting on yourself and what you're truly worth versus working for someone else and living by the worth they establish for you. Done well, you will retire to a reality of lifelong dreams.

For me, I'm in Quarter #3 of my life. I'm doing my best to shorten #4 so that I can reach Overtime as quickly as possible. In order to accomplish that, I need to create generational wealth. And I'm doing the best I can every single day.

My business partner and I created a credible real estate company in Phoenix. Since then, we have opened up multiple locations to help create generational wealth not only for myself but all the agents working with us, and families throughout the valley who want to invest in their future.

Beyond business, I want to travel the world. I have two amazing kids. One of them wants to be a professional soccer player, and the other wants to become a professional dancer. So, I look forward to the day they might go to European academies — as it would require us to relocate across the Atlantic in order to help them realize their goals.

I'm looking forward to our kids finding spouses and having kids of their own one day. That means we'll be grandparents, and my parents always said there's nothing better than spoiling your grandkids. It's even more fun than raising kids!

Beyond their goals, my wife and I want to travel the world for ourselves once our children are old enough to take care of themselves. We want to have the freedom of time and generational wealth so that we can see all the beautiful places that have been created for us.

As I finished arranging the rough draft of this anthology, my wife got promoted to CEO and President of her insurance company. She's worth over 15 years of self-investing, as well as investments made by great mentors (like her mother), colleagues, and business partners. And now she's stepping up to the highest position in her company! I look forward to supporting her in every possible facet so that she can hit her ultimate goals.

Nevertheless, our goals are independent, and they do not rely on pension plans or the government. It's all about investing now for your future — investing back into yourself. Done correctly, you become your own bank creating generational wealth for you and generations to come.

Professionally, I want to develop multiple offices and branches for the brokerage. Ultimately, this will allow me to develop the next generation of professionals. I want to coach and mentor many young professionals who also want to invest in themselves and build generational wealth for years to come.

I've been coached by some of the best in the world. Early in life, my dad was one of my soccer coaches. My mom was also a coach of mine on being a great human being, how to respect people, and how to reach my potential in sports, family, love, and giving back.

Today, my personal business coach helps me in continuing to grow and reach my total potential. For my wife, during her third quarter, she and her company hired an amazing coach who helps her reach her highest potential. My wife is a star, and I love growing in life with her and learning how to further the investments we make into ourselves and others. If you haven't already, I hope you find a partner who accomplishes the same with you.

I'm very passionate about self-investing and investing in others. As many helped me see how I'm a number one asset, I want to do the same for the next generation and pass it forward to as many people as possible who want to enjoy their journey. To follow me on and learn more about my journey, you can stay up to date at www.alwaysaheadseries.com

Our life journey can seem impossible sometimes, especially when we believe that we're alone. There will be times when you're younger and you're not sure which path to choose. Remember, the hardest path to choose is usually the correct path to take.

When we're younger, it's very easy to get derailed. It's easy to be a follower. It's hard to be a leader. I encourage you to find mentors, coaches, and colleagues who can see your true potential and will support you with what we call unconditional love through challenges and success. This will help you reach your truest potential.

I also encourage you to find stories of people who are experiencing this kind of journey. As of now, you've read 12 different stories by 12 different authors of different backgrounds, facing 12 different challenges. And now all these amazing people are giving back to other generations to come. My ambition is to continue finding positive stories and insights to share with and inspire the world.

I could not have done any of this without the amazing people from my childhood. When I was born in the Soviet Union, my parents took a big risk by leaving everything, the only country and language they knew. We came to America when I was only three years old in 1979. They let my sister and me follow our dreams, and they encouraged us to hit our highest potential.

Today, I have an amazing wife who supports me through my growth. With her beside me, I remain encouraged to reach my highest potential. All I ask is that you do the same with your life as you go forward. Thank you so much for reading this book. I hope you've enjoyed it, and I look forward to hearing about your legend in the future.

ABOUT THE AUTHOR

 Born in Ukraine, Oleg Bortman moved to the United States in 1979 as his family sought the American Dream.

Oleg studied biology at York College and upon graduation began working in pharmaceutical sales. He was a Regional Sales Director for a Fortune 100 pharmaceutical company for several years.

However, deep down, Oleg knew his true passion was, and is, real estate. He bought his first investment property in 1999 and quickly became captivated with the entire real estate market. He expanded his portfolio from New Jersey to Nevada and then on to Arizona, quickly seeing his return on investments.

When Oleg moved out West, he realized he didn't just want to be an investor, he wanted to give other people the same opportunities he has had. He loves working not only with buyers but with sellers and investors as well. Oleg has been in real estate for over ten years, and it continues to be his dream career.

84009399R00085